NEW DIRECTIONS FOR STUDENT SERVICES

Margaret J. Barr, *Northwestern Uni*
EDITOR-IN-CHIEF

M. Lee Upcraft, *The Pennsylvania Sι*
ASSOCIATE EDITOR

Developing Student Government Leadership

Melvin C. Terrell
Northeastern Illinois University

Michael J. Cuyjet
University of Louisville

EDITORS

Number 66, Summer 1994

JOSSEY-BASS PUBLISHERS
San Francisco

DEVELOPING STUDENT GOVERNMENT LEADERSHIP
Melvin C. Terrell, Michael J. Cuyjet (eds.)
New Directions for Student Services, no. 66
Margaret J. Barr, Editor-in-Chief
M. Lee Upcraft, Associate Editor

Microfilm copies of issues and articles are available in 16mm and 35mm, as well as microfiche in 105mm, through University Microfilms Inc., 300 North Zeeb Road, Ann Arbor, Michigan 48106-1346.

LC 85-644751   ISSN 0164-7970   ISBN 0-7879-9972-5

NEW DIRECTIONS FOR STUDENT SERVICES is part of The Jossey-Bass Higher and Adult Education Series and is published quarterly by Jossey-Bass Inc., Publishers, 350 Sansome Street, San Francisco, California 94104-1342. Second-class postage paid at San Francisco, California, and at additional mailing offices. POSTMASTER: Send address changes to New Directions for Student Services, Jossey-Bass Inc., Publishers, 350 Sansome Street, San Francisco, California 94104-1342.

SUBSCRIPTIONS for 1994 cost $47.00 for individuals and $62.00 for institutions, agencies, and libraries.

EDITORIAL CORRESPONDENCE should be sent to the Editor-in-Chief, Margaret J. Barr, 633 Clark Street, 2-219, Evanston, Illinois 60208-1103.

Cover photograph by Wernher Krutein/PHOTOVAULT © 1990.

Manufactured in the United States of America. Nearly all Jossey-Bass books, jackets, and periodicals are printed on recycled paper that contains at least 50 percent recycled waste, including 10 percent postconsumer waste. Many of our materials are also printed with vegetable-based inks; during the printing process, these inks emit fewer volatile organic compounds (VOCs) than petroleum-based inks. VOCs contribute to the formation of smog.

CONTENTS

EDITORS' NOTES

A truly "collegiate" form of governance in American colleges and universities involves a sharing relationship among faculty, administrators, and students in institutional decision making, problem solving, and goal setting and in accepting responsibility for the day-to-day and long-range functioning of the institutions. To achieve such shared participation, administration and faculty must invest in student participation.

Such an investment, while requiring both an attitudinal shift for many administrators and a clear effort to educate and develop student leaders in the processes of institutional governance, would pay several different dividends. First, when student leaders are given training and experience in collegiate governance, their education and development are enhanced greatly. Second, student leaders, as representatives of their constituents, can provide a vital resource in the formation of effective institutional policy. Third, student participation in shared governance affords greater acceptability of and support for policy decisions.

The most apparent vehicle for identifying students for participation in college or university governance is through the positional leadership in student government. As a group of student leaders formally selected to represent the issues, concerns, and interests of the entire student body, student government has, traditionally, been afforded some degree of authority in extracurricular matters. However, it is our contention that a comprehensive program for development and inclusion of student government leaders is an invaluable resource in more effective governance of almost any institution of higher education.

The purpose of this volume is to offer a guide to student affairs administrators, academic administrators, faculty leaders, student leaders, and instructors in college or university personnel preparation programs to the understanding and development of astute, enlightened, involved student government leaders as fully participating members of institutional governance. To maximize this guidance, we have included a broad range of perspectives on the structure of student government and its members.

In Chapter One, George D. Kuh and Jon P. Lund examine the gains students can achieve from participation in student government, as described in recent research literature. They also present examples of the benefits that students reported in interviews conducted with 149 seniors at twelve institutions.

In Chapter Two, Dennis C. Golden and Harriet L. Schwartz examine the relationship between senior student affairs officers and student government leaders. They explore the student affairs officer's perspective on the significance of student government, the dynamics of student government from the student leader's perspective, and the characteristics of an ethical relationship among these people that is effective and beneficial to all parties.

In Chapter Three, James A. Gold and Thomas J. Quatroche look at the difference between transactional and transformational leadership characteristics and examine the benefits of transformational leadership principles for student government participants. They also present a model curriculum for student affairs staff, including learning goals and teaching strategies.

In Chapter Four, Tony Chambers and Christine E. Phelps explore the notion of student activism and community involvement as forms of leadership and development. While examining the history of campus activism as well as current issues and concerns, they discuss the contemporary and emerging roles and status of student activism in institutional governance.

In Chapter Five, Bruce D. Lavant and Melvin C. Terrell look at the participation of African American, Asian American, and Hispanic students in student government, paying particular attention to the roles that ethnic minority students are relegated in the structure of student government. They also present the findings from a survey of the attitudes and beliefs of ethnic minority students about their involvement in student government and their authority in student government issues.

In Chapter Six, Michael J. Cuyjet looks at the various services provided by student governments to their campus communities. He also reports the results of a representative, nationwide survey of more than two hundred schools on the services provided by student governments. In addition to identifying the kinds of services provided, respondents—both participants in student government and students who were not involved in positional leadership—expressed how effectively they felt student government achieved the goals of those services.

In Chapter Seven, Dudley B. Woodard, Jr., presents a vision of student government leadership in the future. He looks at societal issues and demographic shifts that will take place by the year 2002 and proposes leadership paradigm shifts that will be necessary to meet the needs of campuses and students in the twenty-first century. He then presents his Leadership 2002 model.

In the final chapter, we offer a summary of and conclusions about the central themes of the volume. We also present an annotated bibliography of selected works that the authors found useful in framing their ideas.

Students, particularly those involved in student government, are an important resource as well as a significant force to reckon with in today's colleges and universities. The effective inclusion of student government leaders in the decision-making affairs of the institution can benefit the entire higher education community.

Melvin C. Terrell
Michael J. Cuyjet
Editors

MELVIN C. TERRELL *is vice president for student affairs and professor of counselor education at Northeastern Illinois University, Chicago. He was a 1993–1994 American Council on Education Fellow at Florida State University.*

MICHAEL J. CUYJET *is associate professor in the Department of Educational and Counseling Psychology at the University of Louisville, Louisville, Kentucky. A former student affairs practitioner, he has served in campus activities and general student affairs capacities at several universities.*

*The benefits associated with involvement in campus governance are
examined and implications for enhancing student learning through
participation in governance structures and processes are discussed.*

What Students Gain from Participating
in Student Government

George D. Kuh, Jon P. Lund

Assertions abound about the value of student involvement in institutional governance. Several years ago, college and university presidents said that a more
active student government was one of the ways to improve the quality of campus life (Carnegie Foundation for the Advancement of Teaching, 1990). An
inactive student government, on the other hand, "closes a main avenue of
involvement—a road that encourages identification with the college and
involvement with ideas" (Clark and Trow, 1966, pp. 51–52). While the value
of student participation in governance to institutional vitality is generally well
recognized, the evidence in terms of benefits to the individual student is largely
anecdotal. Given the interest in outcomes assessment (Ewell, 1988), what students gain from their leadership experience warrants attention.

The purpose of this chapter is to examine the benefits associated with participation in student government. First, the related literature is summarized.
Then, the personal changes that student leaders attribute to their participation
in campus governance are presented. Implications are discussed for student
affairs professionals who are seeking ways to enhance student learning through
participation in campus governance.

What the Literature Notes About the Benefits of
Involvement in Campus Governance

The research on the impact of college or university life on students is unequiv-
ocal: learning and personal development are enhanced when students are more
actively engaged in educationally purposeful out-of-class activities (Astin,

1977, 1984, 1985, 1992; Bowen, 1977; Boyer, 1987; Chickering, 1969; Feldman and Newcomb, 1969; Kuh, 1981; Light, 1992; Pace, 1979, 1990; Pascarella and Terenzini, 1991; Study Group on the Conditions of Excellence in American Higher Education, 1984). For example, more than 70 percent of what students learn during college is attributed to out-of-class experiences (Wilson, 1966). Moffatt (1989, p. 58) found that "for about 40 percent of students, the do-it-yourself side of college [what took place outside the classroom] was the most significant educational experience."

Involvement takes many forms, ranging from joining a social club to playing first clarinet in the touring concert band, to writing for the student newspaper, to collaborating with a faculty member on a research project, to competing in intercollegiate athletics. Involvement in campus governance implies student participation in a wide variety of purposeful and meaningful leadership activities, such as policy and decision making and conflict resolution. Relatively little is known, however, about what students gain from student government leadership positions.

Two streams of inquiries are pertinent: studies that include a student government leadership role as one of several experiences that contribute to student learning and personal development and studies that focus almost exclusively on the student government leadership experience. The first stream of studies has relied on data collected under the auspices of the Cooperative Institutional Research Program (CIRP) (Astin, 1977, 1985, 1992). Astin (1977, p. 224) reported that involvement in student government was "associated with greater-than-average increases in political liberalism, hedonism, and artistic interests." He also noted that participation in campus governance was positively related to satisfaction with peer relations and a need for status. A student government role was negatively related, however, to satisfaction with the intellectual climate of the campus. In his most recent study, Astin (1992) found that election to a student office was positively related to students' self-reported gains in leadership ability.

In other studies that used CIRP data (Astin and Kent, 1983; Ethington, Smart, and Pascarella, 1988; Pascarella, Ethington, and Smart, 1988; Pascarella, Smart, Ethington, and Nettles, 1987; Smart, 1986; Smart and Pascarella, 1986; Stoecker, Pascarella, and Wolfe, 1988), campus governance roles were broadly defined to include serving as president of one or more student organizations or as a member of a university or departmental committee. These and other items (for example, had a major part in a play and won a varsity letter) comprise scales variously called social integration, collegiate experiences, or social leadership experiences. The results from such scales are difficult to interpret because it is not possible to determine clearly which experiences contributed to various outcomes of college or university life. Nonetheless, tentative conclusions can be drawn about the direct and indirect effects of involvement in campus governance on occupational choice, humanitarian interests, self-esteem, self-concept, and persistence.

A direct effect stipulates a relationship between variables, such as participation in student government and satisfaction with the institution, that is not mediated or influenced by other variables, such as achievement test scores or contact with faculty. An indirect effect, however, is transmitted through or mediated by one or more variables. For example, holding a student government leadership position may have an important indirect effect on persistence by influencing the student's overall sense of satisfaction with the institution. In this instance, the indirect influence is participation in student government affecting satisfaction, and satisfaction directly influencing persistence. As Pascarella and Terenzini (1991) noted, many of the effects of college or university are, or could be, indirect.

With this direct-indirect contrast in mind, the findings of the first stream of studies can be summarized as follows: Participation in campus governance has (1) a significant direct effect on women's choice of science occupations (Ethington, Smart, and Pascarella, 1988), no direct effects on occupational status for either professional or nonprofessional occupations, and significant indirect effects on both professional and nonprofessional occupations (Smart, 1986); (2) a significant positive direct effect on the humanitarian values of black men, white men, and white women (the effect for black women was positive also, but not statistically significant; serving on a university or departmental committee was particularly important for white women) and an indirect effect on increasing the likelihood of a student's choice of a social service occupation (Pascarella, Ethington, and Smart, 1988); (3) a significant positive effect on students' perceived leadership competence (Astin, 1992) and on academic, leadership, and social self-esteem of white women (Astin and Kent, 1983); (4) a significant positive direct effect on the social self-concept of black men, white men, and women, on the academic self-concept of black men (Pascarella, Smart, Ethington, and Nettles, 1987), and on students' academic, social, and artistic self-concept (Smart and Pascarella, 1986) and a positive indirect influence on the social self-concept of white women (Pascarella, Smart, Ethington, and Nettles, 1987); and (5) a positive direct effect on the persistence of white men, black men, and white women (Stoecker, Pascarella, and Wolfe, 1988).

Three studies comprise the second stream of research that examines the specific outcomes attributed to holding a student government position. Schwartz (1991) examined the short- and long-term impact on student leaders of experiencing a campus controversy. The six leaders participating in the study were members of either student government or student newspaper editorial boards, during a period of time when the president of their institution was accused of unethical conduct. Schwartz found that the short-term effects included increased stress levels, heightened awareness of ethical issues and dilemmas, and increased use of coping strategies. Respondents also reported such long-term effects as an enhanced sense of moral awareness and personal responsibility.

To examine the perceived long-term impact of participating in campus governance, Schuh and Laverty (1983) studied graduates of three different types of institutions (a women's institution, a church-related institution, and a large public institution) who held various leadership roles, such as student body, senior class, or interfraternity council officers. Respondents reported that their leadership experience had little or no subsequent influence on their lives in areas such as marriage, child rearing, relationships with other family members, religious activities, or further educational experiences. However, many reported that their leadership roles had a significant influence on the relationships that they developed with individuals beyond their family and with their involvement in civic organizations. They also attributed the greatest impact of their leadership roles to their development of skills in areas such as leadership, decision making, planning, organizing, and teamwork. These findings were the same for both men and women at all three types of institutions.

Downey, Bosco, and Silver (1984) studied the perceived long-term effects of participation in student government by comparing responses of people who had held student government positions between 1967 and 1979 with the responses of their counterparts who had not held such positions. Contrary to Schuh and Laverty (1983), they did not find that involvement in student government had long-term effects, other than former student leaders' reports of a higher level of satisfaction with choice of vocation.

What Students Say About the Benefits of Participating in Student Government

The rest of this chapter is based on interviews with seniors at a dozen institutions, conducted during the 1988–1989 academic year under the auspices of the College Experiences Study (Kuh, Schuh, Whitt, and Associates, 1991). Unlike studies that ask students to reflect on specific experiences, such as student body president or student government membership as one of many potential social leadership roles, the interviews asked students to describe how they had changed during college or university enrollment, and then to identify the experiences to which these changes could be attributed. This kind of approach elicits a more accurate account of the relationships between experiences and outcomes because it does not force students to concentrate on an activity or role, such as student government leader, which creates an obligation among respondents to please the interviewer by identifying changes that may not necessarily be attributable to the experiences in question.

Outcomes Taxonomy. Kuh's (1993) outcomes taxonomy (see Appendix to this chapter) was used to categorize the benefits reported by student government leaders. This taxonomy includes fourteen categories of outcomes typically associated with college or university attendance (Pascarella and Terenzini, 1991): self-awareness, autonomy, confidence, altruism, reflective thought, social competence, practical competence, knowledge acquisition, academic skills, application of knowledge, aesthetic appreciation, vocational competence, sense of purpose, and a miscellaneous "other" category (for example, changes in physical features). The transcripts were analyzed to determine the specific experiences to which students attributed these benefits. More than twenty experiences were identified, including interactions with peers, academic requirements, faculty contact, work, volunteerism, writing for the student newspaper or yearbook, travel, fraternity and sorority life, and residence hall life (Kuh, 1992). The following discussion focuses on the benefits students attributed to their participation in campus governance.

Survey Respondents. Of the 149 seniors interviewed, 26 held some form of student government position, such as student body president, elected student representative to the campus governing council, or another position in student government. The group included 11 men and 15 women, approximately the same proportions as were in the total group of 69 men and 80 women. The race and ethnicity of those involved in student government also was representative of the group as a whole. The vast majority (92 percent) were traditional age (eighteen to twenty-three).

Synopsis of Pertinent Findings. When participation in student government was correlated with the fourteen outcomes from the Kuh taxonomy, the only statistically significant result was a .22 relationship with gains in practical competence. None of the other correlations came even close to statistical significance. The next most powerful relationship was a negative correlation (−.13) with altruism. However, in comparing the benefits reported by respondents who were involved in student government with the reports of their counterparts who did not hold such positions, we found that the relationships between student government experiences and outcomes are complicated.

Table 1.1. A Comparison of Outcomes Associated with Student Government and Other Experiences

Outcome	Student Government			Other Experiences			Row Total	
	N	Row %	Column %	N	Row %	Column %	N	Column %
Self-awareness	2	1.2	3.1	161	98.8	8.4	163	8.2
Autonomy	3	2.0	4.6	148	98.0	7.7	151	7.6
Confidence	6	3.2	9.2	183	96.8	9.6	189	9.6
Altruism	6	2.4	9.2	243	97.6	12.7	249	12.6
Reflective thought	4	1.6	6.2	239	98.4	12.5	243	12.3
Social competence	12	4.4	18.5	262	95.6	13.7	274	13.9
Practical competence	25	14.9	38.5	143	85.1	7.5	168	8.5
Knowledge aquisition				154	100	8.1	154	7.8
Academic skills	1	1.1	1.5	91	98.9	4.8	92	4.7
Knowledge application	1	2.2	1.5	45	97.8	2.4	46	2.3
Aesthetic appreciation				20	100	1.0	20	1.0
Vocational competence	2	5.3	3.1	36	94.7	1.9	38	1.9
Sense of purpose	3	3.1	4.6	94	96.9	4.9	97	4.9
Other				94	100	4.9	94	4.8
Total	65		3.3	1,913		96.7	1,978	100

Table 1.1 shows the frequency with which a particular outcome was attributed to involvement in student government or other types of experiences, such as peers, fraternity affairs, faculty interaction, residence halls, athletics, and academic program. The data indicate that some students associated a variety of benefits with participation in student government. The relative contribution that student government experiences made to gains in the respective outcomes categories can be determined by comparing the column percentages with the respective row percentages. For the purpose of these comparisons, percentages of ± 3 were considered similar. For example, participation in student government was associated with the development of confidence about as often as all other types of experiences combined: 9.2 and 9.6 column percentages, respectively, compared with the 9.6 row total percentage. Similar relationships were found for autonomy, sense of purpose, vocational competence, and altruism (although it was negatively correlated with student government). However, student government experiences were, on average, less important compared to other kinds of activities in terms of the development of self-awareness, reflective thought, knowledge acquisition, and aesthetic appreciation.

Most important, perhaps, was that student government experiences were more meaningful, on average, than were other areas of involvement in relation to the development of social and practical competence. Indeed, as mentioned earlier, student government was the single most potent experience associated with the development of practical competence. Almost two-fifths of the outcomes associated with student government were related to practical competence. Thus, participation in student government seems to yield skills that employers indicate are needed for workplace competence: decision making, an understanding and appreciation of fundamental organizational structures and processes, experience with group process and team work (for example, leadership, cooperation, and followership), and writing and oral and visual communication skills (Cappelli, 1992; Tucker, 1992).

To illustrate this point, a traditional-age student at Mount Holyoke College talked about how her involvement in student government contributed to the development of practical and social competence: "I learned about people and getting along with people and technical things like organizing and it has helped my writing skills, having to write letters to the administration or whatever. . . . So as far as learning and student government, that's where I have really become aware of issues like racism and dealt with them by trying to do programming" (Kuh, Schuh, Whitt, and Associates, 1991). Consider, too, how student government influenced the development of practical competence of an African American male student at the University of California, Davis:

> I'm learning a lot just as far as organizational skills, administrative skills, motivating skills, staff development skills, interviewing. . . . I mean, you name it, any area of improvement that a student can actually go through to make him marketable is what I'm going through now. . . . The areas that I needed improve-

ment on were areas I had to focus on and improve. . . . Now I have to be organized—my appointment book, my agenda, everything set. I have to be rolling,
I have to have a filing system. I have to be able to foresee and envision things
coming up . . . look and anticipate what are going to be the hot issues. I'm also
developing speaking skills, how to convey messages. And as far as working on
some of my weaker areas, such as budgeting, we work with a four million dol-
lar budget so it is really not a patty-cake job. We hire for 40 different units so
that is 40 directors [Kuh, Schuh, Whitt, and Associates, 1991].

An Earlham College senior reported similar benefits: "On the faculty affairs
committee you actually help decide who gets hired, who gets promoted. I've
learned some leadership skills and the ability to work with groups—how to
focus a group on a certain task and how to—in Quaker terms—'get a sense of
the Meeting' where you get a general feel for what people are thinking and try
to draw it out of them and bring the group to consensus which is where every-
body agrees on a certain aspect of the decision involved" (Kuh, Schuh, Whitt,
and Associates, 1991).

Participation in student government also can contribute to the development of self-confidence and self-esteem, as illustrated by the Hispanic student
body president at Wichita State University: "I have a lot a more self-worth
because I was in the executive cabinet of the Vice President of Minority Affairs.
I also got involved with the committee in my public relations major called
'Visions' that was significant because I helped formulate a public relations campaign for a company and saw how it related to my classwork. . . . I learned that
I can bite my tongue . . . and that a fool blurts out but a wise man thinks
before he speaks" (Kuh, Schuh, Whitt, and Associates, 1991).

As other studies have indicated (for example, Schuh and Laverty, 1983),
college graduates who were involved in campus governance often become
involved in civic affairs later in life. Even though participation in student government was negatively correlated with the development of altruism, at the
same time student government had a powerful, enhancing influence on
humanitarian attitudes for certain individuals. Consider the three respondents
who described a heightened sense of awareness of the needs of others that
derived from working in student government (Kuh, Schuh, Whitt, and Associates, 1991):

Last year we got the sense that athletes were being stereotyped. That when people thought of an athlete they tended to think of them as not as intelligent and
not as capable. That precipitated people beginning to look around and observe
in the dining room that athletes tended to sit by themselves and other people
said nothing to them. That is also true for racial groups and ethnic minorities.
And so we decided that this should be a topic for weekly meetings of students
for all students. I walked into that meeting and usually our attendance is some-
where around 10 to 20 people. Well, there were 150 athletes at this meeting. It
just kind of blew me away because I never had to try to "get a sense of the Meet-

ing" with 150 people participating. So, as you can imagine, working with this group that size gave me a lot of confidence and empowered me to see that change is possible and that students can make a difference at an institution.

> I am more confident. . . . I feel like I can think on my own—not something I've always had. . . . I have more faith in my fellow students than I did. . . . Good things will happen. If someone isn't working on a cause this year, they probably will be next year. . . . I feel a greater urgency to contribute to my society more than I did. . . . I see that to be a really successful person, I need to help those less fortunate. I need to work to change the legislation. I feel like that is something that has come about that I will keep pursuing after college. . . . I count that as a gift.

> I met a vast majority of people, different types of people. I deal with international students more than I ever have and I see how their way of life is very different and that if I were to go to Pakistan or Saudi Arabia or Israel, there's really no way I could truly understand those people because I don't think like they do. And I have a better appreciation for their struggle in getting an education here when our way of life and our language is so different.

Exposure to views of others with more life experience is important according to a Grinnell College senior: "I've had a very good, rich experience with some of the administrators here. I have a very good relationship with the president and I appreciate that fact, because I have seen how he views things and how he must view things in the larger context than a student context and I've learned a lot from that interaction" (Kuh, Schuh, Whitt, and Associates, 1991). An Earlham College senior offered a similar sentiment: "You get involved with weekly face-to-face meetings with administrators on such committees as the budget committee where you participate along with other faculty and administrators deciding the nature of funding for all the departments. It is not only an educational experience but it teaches you how things work at an institution and gives you a very large sense of responsibility" (Kuh, Schuh, Whitt, and Associates, 1991).

Implications

Students' attributions about the experiences associated with their learning in college confirm what has been espoused frequently about the value of participating in student government. Student government demands that students learn how to work with, through, and for people who are different from or similar to themselves. "Programs that bring young potential leaders together for a shared experience have an effect over and above the nature of the particular program. The fact of having been singled out has a motivating effect and contact with peers may have a considerable impact" (Gardner, 1990, p. 167). Viewed from this perspective, student government experiences probably have numerous indirect as well as direct influences on student learning and personal development. Students who are actively involved in student government are more likely to engage in other activities that contribute to learning and personal development, such as meeting people from different backgrounds, traveling, and writing memoranda and letters.

Certain outcomes that are thought to be associated with student government, for example, self-awareness and enhanced appreciation and concern for the welfare of others, were not emphasized by many students in our study. Recall that Pascarella, Ethington, and Smart (1988) concluded that social leadership experiences were the single most important factor contributing to the development of humanitarian interests. It is possible that some respondents in our study came to their respective colleges or universities concerned about the welfare of others, a personality characteristic that encouraged them to pursue campus governance leadership positions. It was disappointing, however, that relatively few students pointed to their involvement in student government as instrumental to a deepening of their humanitarian interests. Student affairs staff should periodically remind students as well as colleagues that knowing oneself and being committed to enhancing the quality of life for others characterize servant leaders in all walks of life (Greenleaf, 1977) and are qualities worth cultivating.

Only a few times did students mention that student government experiences were associated with reflective thought (see Table 1.1). Here is an opportunity to help student leaders gain more from their experiences by asking them to think about how their responsibilities can make a difference in the quality of campus life as well as in their own personal development. Students typically exhibit gains in areas in which they expend effort and that their institutions emphasize (Astin, 1992; Pace, 1990; Pascarella and Terenzini, 1991). If dialogue between student government advisers and student leaders requires self-reflection, gains in these areas will accrue. Such behaviors will have a positive influence on the quality of campus life because as student leaders become more reflective, they will become more intellectually competent, which will improve their ability to govern effectively.

The results also suggest that campus governance is not used very often as a vehicle for applying what students learn in the classroom. Therefore, student affairs staff should routinely ask students to think about and use what they are learning in their classes. At the same time, classroom instructors could ask students to draw examples from their student government leadership experiences of how material presented in their classes can be used to explain what takes place in campus governance.

Conclusion

Participation in campus governance is linked to desirable outcomes for individual students as well as to positive contributions to the welfare of the campus community. For example, performance of specific tasks demanded in campus governance, such as organizing, planning, managing, and decision making, results in the development of practical competence and confidence from working with people who are different from oneself. Campus governance also offers numerous, often untapped opportunities for synthesizing and integrating material presented in classes, laboratories, and studios. More students must be encouraged to take advantage of these opportunities, which can enhance their learning and personal development.

At the same time, institutions must expand the number of opportunities for student involvement in campus governance. Given the benefits that accrue to students through their involvement in governance, it follows that more opportunities lead to more benefits for more students. As Boyer (1987, p. 246) observed, not only should students be encouraged to understand how decisions are made at their institutions but they should be asked, indeed expected, to participate as campus citizens as well. If habits of good citizenship are not cultivated when students are in college—if they are kept at arm's length—it is not surprising that later in life these same people remain detached from civic life.

This chapter celebrates the contributions to learning and personal development made by participation in campus governance. But it is important to note that active engagement in other areas of campus life also is associated with benefits similar to those of student government. Although there are a finite number of student government positions on any campus, many more opportunities for learning exist through active participation in the life of the institution. Thus, student government leaders, and those who work with them, should encourage all students to take advantage of as many of these opportunities as possible.

Appendix: Taxonomy of Outcomes Reported by Seniors

1. Self-awareness (includes self-examination and spirituality)
2. Autonomy and self-directedness (includes taking initiative and responsibility for one's own affairs and learning, movement from dependent to independent thinking)
3. Confidence and self-worth (includes esteem and self-respect)
4. Altruism (includes interest in the welfare of others, awareness of and empathy and respect for needs of others, tolerance and acceptance of people from racial, ethnic, cultural, and religious backgrounds different from one's own)
5. Reflective thought (includes critical thinking, synthesizing information and experiences, seeing connections between thinking and experiences, seeing different points of view, and examining one's own thinking)
6. Social competence (includes capacity for intimacy, working with others, teamwork, leadership, dealing with others, assertiveness, flexibility, public speaking, communication, and patience)
7. Practical competence (includes decision-making ability, organizational skills such as time management, budgeting, and dealing with systems and bureaucracies)
8. Knowledge acquisition (includes academic and course-related learning, content mastery)
9. Academic skills (includes learning how to study, to write, and to conduct independent research)
10. Application of knowledge (includes relating theory to practice and using skills learned in the classroom, laboratory, library and so on in other areas of life, such as using political science theory and research methods when working in a law office)
11. Aesthetic appreciation (includes appreciation for cultural matters as in the arts, literature, and theater and for aesthetic qualities of nature)
12. Vocational competence (includes acquiring attitudes, behaviors, and skills related to postcollege employment)
13. Sense of purpose (includes clarifying life goals and the work one will do after college, sometimes by discovering what one is not well suited to do)
14. Other (includes movement from conservative to liberal attitudes, or vice versa, change in physical features, growing apart from a spouse, and so on)

Source: Kuh, 1993.

References

Astin, A. W. *Four Critical Years: Effects of College on Beliefs, Attitudes, and Knowledge.* San Francisco: Jossey-Bass, 1977.

Astin, A. W. "Student Involvement: A Developmental Theory for Higher Education." *Journal of College Student Personnel,* 1984, *25,* 297–308.

Astin, A. W. *Achieving Educational Excellence: A Critical Assessment of Priorities and Practices in Higher Education.* San Francisco: Jossey-Bass, 1985.

Astin, A. W. *What Matters in College?: Four Critical Years Revisited.* San Francisco: Jossey-Bass, 1992.

Astin, H. S., and Kent, L. "Gender Roles in Transition: Research and Policy Implications for Higher Education." *Journal of Higher Education,* 1983, *54,* 309–324.

Bowen, H. R. *Investment in Learning: The Individual and Social Value of American Higher Education.* San Francisco: Jossey-Bass, 1977.

Boyer, E. L. *College: The Undergraduate Experience in America.* New York: HarperCollins, 1987.

Cappelli, P. "College, Students, and the Workplace: Assessing Performance to Improve the Fit." *Change,* 1992, *24* (6), 55–61.

Carnegie Foundation for the Advancement of Teaching. *Campus Life: In Search of Community.* Princeton, N.J.: Princeton University Press, 1990.

Chickering, A. W. *Education and Identity.* San Francisco: Jossey-Bass, 1969.

Clark, B. R., and Trow, M. "The Organizational Context." In T. M. Newcomb and E. K. Wilson (eds.), *College Peer Groups: Problems and Prospects for Research.* Hawthorne, N.Y.: Aldine, 1966.

Downey, R. G., Bosco, P. J., and Silver, E. M. "Long-Term Outcomes of Participation in Student Government." *Journal of College Student Personnel,* 1984, *25,* 245–250.

Ethington, C. A., Smart, J. C., and Pascarella, E. T. "Influences on Women's Entry into Male-Dominated Occupations." *Higher Education,* 1988, *17,* 545–562.

Ewell, P. T. "Outcomes, Assessment, and Academic Improvement: In Search of Usable Knowledge." In J. Smart (ed.), *Higher Education: Handbook of Theory and Research.* Vol. 4. New York: Agathon, 1988.

Feldman, K. A., and Newcomb, T. M. *The Impact of College on Students.* San Francisco: Jossey-Bass, 1969.

Gardner, J. W. *On Leadership.* New York: Free Press, 1990.

Greenleaf, R. K. *Servant Leadership: A Journey into the Nature of Legitimate Power and Greatness.* New York: Paulist Press, 1977.

Kuh, G. D. *Indices of Quality in the Undergraduate Experience.* ASHE-ERIC Higher Education Research Reports, no. 4. Washington, D.C.: Association for the Study of Higher Education, 1981.

Kuh, G. D. "The Other Curriculum: Out-of-Class Experiences Associated with Student Learning and Personal Development." Paper presented at the annual meeting of the Association for the Study of Higher Education, Minneapolis, Nov. 1992.

Kuh, G. D. "In Their Own Words: What Students Learn Outside the Classroom." *American Educational Research Journal,* 1993, *30,* 277–304.

Kuh, G. D., Schuh, J. H., Whitt, E. J., and Associates. *Involving Colleges: Successful Approaches to Fostering Student Learning and Development Outside the Classroom.* San Francisco: Jossey-Bass, 1991.

Light, R. J. *The Harvard Assessment Seminars: Explorations with Students and Faculty About Teaching, Learning, and Student Life (Second Report).* Cambridge, Mass.: Graduate School of Education and Kennedy School of Government, Harvard University, 1992.

Moffatt, M. *Coming of Age in New Jersey: College and American Culture.* New Brunswick, N.J.: Rutgers University Press, 1989.

Pace, C. R. *Measuring Outcomes of College: Fifty Years of Findings and Recommendations for the Future.* San Francisco: Jossey-Bass, 1979.

Pace, C. R. *The Undergraduates: A Report of Their Activities and Progress in College in the 1980s.* Los Angeles: Center for the Study of Evaluation, University of California, 1990.

Pascarella, E. T., Ethington, C. A., and Smart, J. C. "The Influence of College on Humanitarian/Civic Involvement Values." *Journal of Higher Education,* 1988, *59,* 412–437.

Pascarella, E. T., Smart, J. C., Ethington, C. A., and Nettles, M. T. "The Influence of College on Self-Concept: A Consideration of Race and Gender Differences." *American Educational Research Journal,* 1987, *24,* 49–77.

Pascarella, E. T., and Terenzini, P. T. *How College Affects Students: Findings and Insights from Twenty Years of Research.* San Francisco: Jossey-Bass, 1991.

Schuh, J. H., and Laverty, M. "The Perceived Long-Term Influence of Holding a Significant Student Leadership Position." *Journal of College Student Personnel,* 1983, *24,* 28–32.

Schwartz, H. L. "An Interview Study of Former Student Leaders' Perceptions of an Ethical Conflict Involving the College or University President." *Journal of College Student Development,* 1991, *32,* 447–454.

Smart, J. C. "College Effects on Occupational Status Attainment." *Research in Higher Education,* 1986, *24,* 73–95.

Smart, J. C., and Pascarella, E. T. "Self-Concept Development and Educational Degree Attainment." *Higher Education,* 1986, *15,* 3–15.

Stoecker, J., Pascarella, E. T., and Wolfe, L. M. "Persistence in Higher Education: A Nine-Year Test of a Theoretical Model." *Journal of College Student Development,* 1988, *29,* 196–209.

Study Group on the Conditions of Excellence in American Higher Education. *Involvement in Learning: Realizing the Potential of American Higher Education.* Washington, D.C.: Government Printing Office, 1984.

Tucker, R. W. "National Certification of Workplace Competence for College Graduates." *Adult Assessment Forum,* 1992, 2 (3), 3–5, 10, 12.

Wilson, E. K. "The Entering Student: Attributes and Agents of Change." In T. Newcomb and E. Wilson (eds.), *College Peer Groups: Problems and Prospects for Research.* Hawthorne, N.Y.: Aldine, 1966.

GEORGE D. KUH is professor of higher education at Indiana University, Bloomington.

JON P. LUND is a doctoral student at Indiana University, Bloomington, and has worked with student governments for the past seven years at a variety of institutions.

The senior student affairs officer who is invested in encouraging and maintaining an involved campus community must support a strong student government.

Building an Ethical and Effective Relationship with Student Government Leaders

Dennis C. Golden, Harriet L. Schwartz

Among the many vital relationships that senior student affairs officers (SSAOs) must develop on campus, few are as important as the relationship with student government leaders. This relationship is important for the SSAO's effectiveness on campus as an administrator and as an educator (Sandeen, 1991), providing essential opportunities to establish ties with the student community and to teach both formally and by example.

Student government is essential to the campus community. Replicating our nation's representative government process, student government provides students with opportunities to view a political governing body in action and realize the importance of voting and participation. Officeholders and other involved students develop leadership skills and knowledge. In short, student government offers many of the opportunities and lessons that Morse (1989) indicated are necessary for teaching students to serve and be good citizens. Moreover, an active student government is vital to the preservation of the campus community, as described by the Carnegie Foundation for the Advancement of Teaching (1990), that is, a community that is purposeful, open, just, disciplined, caring, and celebrative. The importance of student involvement in institutional governance, in terms of both maintaining a strong campus community and providing learning experiences, is also affirmed by Kuh, Schuh, Whitt, and Associates (1991).

This chapter provides frameworks for understanding student government and student government leaders and advice for working with these student leaders. More specifically, we provide an overview of the history of student government, as well as a portrait of the dynamics of student government leadership and organizations. Then we explore the working relationship between SSAOs and student government officers. The chapter concludes with a code of ethics.

History of Student Government

Literature on the history of student governments is limited, however Horowitz (1987) explored the early development of student governing groups. She suggested that administrations created a system of student governance to increase their control over their student bodies. According to the literature, U.S. colleges and universities began developing student government organizations between 1900 and 1920 (Horowitz, 1987; Smith, 1986; Tarbell, 1937). Horowitz (1987) described the role of early student governments, noting that the early student governments consisted of student-elected officers with little power. These organizations were allowed to contribute ideas regarding campus governance, but they had minimal decision-making authority. Student government leaders were expected to influence other students on campus. Student government was part of the effort to harness college or university life to official ends.

In 1906–1907, the Carnegie Institute of Technology established a board of student activities, which supervised a number of student organizations. The board eventually managed the fund created by the activity fee, which was established in 1909. In 1917, a student council was formed "to control . . . the government angle on student life involving the election of senate and class officers, as well as the management of matters that required joint action of the entire student body" (Tarbell, 1937, p. 234). In 1923, the board of student activities and the student council were merged, and the new organization managed the previously held responsibilities of both organizations, as well as "the setting up of the annual calendar for social events, the supervision of freshman regulations, the carrying on of traditions and similar duties" (Smith, 1986, p. 94).

At Harvard University, the early student government had connections with the president. Smith (1986) noted that in 1927 President Lowell enlisted student council support in his effort to promote an innovative house plan to students. From the time of his inauguration, President Lowell courted the student council and was pleased to enlist the council's aid.

Horowitz (1987) suggested that a movement to change the role of student governments began in the 1930s when rebels, a group defined as politically active and outside of the mainstream, became increasingly involved in student government. The Jacobin Club at the University of Minnesota, ten or twelve high academic achievers with radical convictions, is an example of rebel influence on student governments. "As they gained control of campus organizations . . . they tried to make student government into a real policy-making body, rather than a puppet of the administration" (Horowitz, 1987, p. 162).

The most significant shift in student involvement and influence vis-à-vis campus governance occurred in the 1960s. Responding to the free speech movement, faculty members and trustees reconsidered the role of students in institutional governance. On some campuses, students became more involved in campus governance through participation in committees, governing boards, and faculty groups. This expanded participation appeared to give students more influence, but the real power remained with the administration (Horowitz, 1987).

This shift to more active and activist student governments impacted the organizations' internal and external operations. Student government representatives became increasingly concerned with one another's politics. In 1961, for example, Howard Phillips, a conservative president of the Harvard Student Council, was forced out of office for his public criticism of the Peace Corps (Smith, 1986). Moreover, on many campuses where unofficial groups began attempting to influence institutional policies and procedures, presidents, SSAOs, and other administrators tried to work closely with recognized student governments. On February 17, 1969, Notre Dame's president, the Rev. Theodore Hesburgh, sent a letter to all students addressing the issue of campus protests. In his letter, Hesburgh noted that the Student Life Council supported his belief that protests were to be considered valid and sometimes necessary, but that normal institutional operation must not be impeded, or the individual rights of any individual abrogated. Any student in violation of this policy would be referred to the disciplinary board established by the Student Life Council (Hesburgh and Reedy, 1990).

By 1970, many in higher education began to acknowledge the importance of student involvement in campus governance, the need for presidents to have a greater appreciation of the role of students in campus governance, and the valuable input from those students involved in governance. McGrath (1970) felt that students' participation in the making of academic policy must be formalized and their contribution regularized so as to involve students as initiators, not as protesters, relative to policy.

Events of the early 1970s, including the killings at Kent State and the end of the Vietnam conflict, led to a changed focus in American society as well as on college campuses. Undergraduates became less focused on political issues and more focused on campus issues. Horowitz (1987, p. 258) cited Arthur Levine's observations that "moved by their sense of entitlement, students created a campus consumer movement. They fought against the raising of fees, restricted library hours, the inability of teaching assistants to speak comprehensible English."

Dynamics of Student Government Leadership

To understand student government leaders (SGLs), one must examine their motivations for getting involved. Although their motivations are as individual and varied as their personalities, in general there are commonalities. Students tend to get involved because they strongly desire to make a difference on campus, they view student government as a significant leadership development opportunity, they wish to further a particular issue or political agenda, or they have been previously uninvolved and suddenly expect that student government will bring them power or visibility on campus. Often, students are motivated by a combination of these reasons, rather than a singular reason. However, most students do have a primary motivating force, and an understanding of this motivation can help the student affairs administrator anticipate SGLs' styles, priorities, and activities.

Desire to Contribute. Some students join student government and ascend to high positions because they are motivated by a strong desire to improve the campus community. This ethic of service seems to be on the increase with the national trend toward increased service, which has included increased service on the high school and postsecondary levels. An increasing number of students entering college have an understanding of their responsibilities to their communities. They are significantly invested in their institutions and in general hold positive views of their schools. While they basically feel good about the institutions, they also hold many ideas on how to improve campus life. These students are eager to get involved beyond their specified student government duties and are often willing to participate in standing communities, search committees, and other campus initiatives. They tend to look more at the potential outcomes of an action or initiative than at the political ramifications but are often also politically aware enough to understand at least some of the political dynamics. While these students are focused primarily on contributing to the campus community, they often view their positions as leadership development opportunities and thus are open to mentoring, leadership training, and other developmental experiences.

Leadership Development Opportunity. Some students see leadership development as the primary benefit of involvement in student government. These students are interested in developing their leadership skills and styles for career and political aspirations. They also tend to be fairly invested in bettering the campus community and often have many ideas and new initiatives; however, they are sometimes more concerned with political dynamics, and the visibility and recognition that success can bring, than with improvements in campus life. Often, they eagerly become involved in committees and other outside work, motivated in part by the connections, visibility, and political engagement that these opportunities bring. These students are mostly interested in leadership development opportunities and may respond positively to mentoring, depending on their own sense of self and perceived need for development and growth.

Commitment to Diversity. Students are becoming increasingly aware of and attentive to the diversity of their immediate and larger communities. They see involvement in student government as a means to contribute to their communities with respect to issues of gender, race, ethnicity, physical ability, and sexual orientation. In addition, many students see student government involvement as an opportunity to engage with students of differing backgrounds and perspectives. These students tend to value opportunities to contribute and grow and thus are often interested in committee work, mentoring opportunities, and training opportunities.

Political Agenda. Occasionally, students who are primarily focused on one issue or are committed to furthering a particular political agenda seek high office in student government. Because of their somewhat limited focus, these students do not tend to be compelled by other issues, or by the need to improve the campus at large. Thus, they often are disinterested in committee work and other involvements unless they pertain to the students' primary issue of concern. In addition, these students typically do not attend to leadership development and thus do not engage in training or mentoring relationships. Sometimes, after a period of involvement, they will develop a broader concern for campuswide issues and their styles and involvements may change.

The Outsider. Occasionally, students who are previously uninvolved in student government will run for the organization's highest office, and win. These students may have found success and popularity in other student organizations (for example, Greek life or ethnically based student groups), and they believe that their earlier successes indicate potential for success in the highest levels of student government. In other cases, previously uninvolved students who find themselves suddenly engaged in an issue, campus politics, or the institution in general believe that they can do a better job than that of students already involved in student government. Many of these students may find difficulty in meeting their goals because they lack knowledge of the student government and institutional systems, politics, and the histories of particular issues and initiatives. Sometimes, however, because these students may be uninvolved in internal organizational politics, they may actually find it easier to accomplish goals than do more entrenched SGLs. These students are often at least somewhat interested in committee work and leadership development opportunities, depending on the agendas they develop as they move into office and their self-perceptions regarding leadership capability and growth potential.

Student Government Power and Operation Within the Campus Context

To understand the internal dynamics of student government, one must examine the focus of an organization and the experience level of its leaders.

External Versus Internal Focus. Consider the primary focus of the student government. Are members of the organization internally focused on the organization? Internal focusing frequently happens either when many members are new and thus just learning their positions or when they are extensively engaged in internal political battles. When the focus is primarily internal, for example, power struggles or rewriting of the constitution, members are probably not unified and their attention and ability to act on external issues and initiatives are low. On the other hand, an experienced membership and leadership are better positioned to address external issues and take action. Moreover, a student government can quickly become unified and action-oriented when members galvanize against a force or situation, which may include the administration, student newspaper, or some other student group.

Coalitions. On some campuses, coalition building within the student government is a frequently pursued strategy. The coalitions tend to develop when students are running for office. Students of several like-minded organizations (for example, Greeks or political groups) will run for positions hoping to gain a broad base of influence over funding or policy decisions. Coalitions may also form later in response to a particular issue or funding decision. Coalition-based student government organizations often remain primarily focused on the issues that motivated the formation of the coalitions. Moreover, the make-up of coalition-based student governments can vary greatly from year to year as issues and funding trends change.

Stressors Faced by Student Government Leaders

SGLs are faced with many of the same stressors encountered by uninvolved students, as well as with difficulties presented by their student government involvement. SGLs also may face additional stressors during a campus controversy.

Stress Associated with Being a Student. Like all other students, SGLs may encounter stressors such as difficulties with academic work, time demands of holding a part-time job, problems with roommates, and family or relationship problems. Because SGLs often appear to be successful, confident, and capable, it is easy to forget that they may be dealing with one or more of a number of difficulties. In addition, SGLs are often aware that they are perceived as a cut above other students, and this may make it more difficult for them to seek help and support.

Stress Generated by Student Government Involvement. SGLs may also face a number of stressors inherent to student government involvement. A major issue for many SGLs is time management; they find their student government work compelling, devote significant time to it, and may eventually fall behind in class work. Some SGLs find it difficult to balance the primary role of being a student with the secondary role of being visible and sometimes powerful leaders on campus. SGLs often interact with a wide range of people, from members of their own organization to administrators. There are many kinds of pressures that may emerge in these interactions, such as officers who do not do their jobs adequately and administrators who pressure SGLs to take a particular stand. SGLs must often deal with being in the spotlight as spokespersons to the administration, through the campus media.

Stress Resulting from a Campus Controversy. Schwartz (1991) found that SGLs on a campus where there is a large-scale controversy, for example, a president accused of harassment or misuse of funds, are likely to experience additional stress. The politics and conflict on a campus are often heightened during controversies. In Schwartz's study, SGLs reported feeling pressure from individuals and groups on campus who opposed their views. In addition, the SGLs became increasingly stressed in their encounters with community and campus media; they were uncomfortable during interviews and often felt as if they were misquoted or misrepresented. Many of these students also became increasingly frustrated because the demands of dealing with the controversy often prevented them from accomplishing previously set academic and organizational goals.

Working Together: Senior Student Affairs Officers and Student Government Leaders

The complexities of the campus and the dynamics among SSAOs, SGLs, other student leaders, and other administrators place many demands on the relationship between SSAOs and SGLs. Sometimes, SSAOs find less than smooth relationships when dealing with multiple, complex matters. The SSAO should never try to shield or co-opt SGLs. To shield them is to weaken their position with their own constituency and to run the risk that the SGLs will be viewed as a puppet government under the control of the faculty, administration, and governing board. An attempt to co-opt them may also lead to disaster because once SGLs realize what is happening, they will turn on the SSAO and make the political climate so intense that the SSAO loses his or her position.

Aside from these extremes, the SSAO must be prepared to mediate between the SGLs and the student newspaper as well as between the SGLs and special interest groups such as the Gay, Lesbian, and Bisexual Alliance, the Greeks, and AHANA (African, Hispanic, Asian, and Native American). These groups are mentioned here not because they traditionally disagree with SGLs but because their needs, issues, concerns, and rights are so strongly advanced that frequently SGLs, especially newly elected ones, are not ready to deal with such demanding agenda items.

Furthermore, the SSAO must understand that he or she is the person who is always in the middle. The president often expects the SSAO to keep students in line, to control them. Moreover, the SSAO is expected to accurately interject student opinions and beliefs into the deliberations of senior administrative staff, the president, and the governing board. To some degree, the SSAO is simultaneously with students, for students, about students, and subject to students. This task is not easy and requires experience, patience, and wisdom. In addition, the SSAO must want to work with and be with students. Anything less than this type of deep and abiding desire will fall far short of what is needed to achieve acceptable professional performance.

If, however, the desire is there, the SSAO and SGLs working together can inform and assist the campus in many ways. According to Bolman and Deal (1991), there are four main frames of reference in which to analyze and make decisions about campus issues: the structural frame, the political frame, the human relations frame, and the symbolic frame. Most often, the administration is focused on the structural and political frames, while the student leaders are more comfortable with the human relations and symbolic frames. Therefore, the SSAO and SGLs can influence campus policy, practices, and procedures by understanding these frames and by flipping the frames back and forth so as to broadly analyze thoughts, concerns, and issues and thereby maximize the discussion, interaction, and review among internal and external communities so that the best possible decisions are made.

Ethical and Effective Relationship Between the Senior Student Affairs Officer and Student Government Leaders

Sandeen (1991) stated that the SSAO must be a major campus leader who fulfills the administrative roles and responsibilities of manager, mediator, and educator. In fulfilling these functions, however, the SSAO must recognize that in the real world of professional practice, student affairs presents an ongoing variety of situations and circumstances that entail ethical dilemmas. Canon (1993) identified the recognition that an ethical problem exists as the most critical barrier to maintaining high-quality performance relative to ethical practices in student affairs. Too often, self-interest, even in the pursuit of laudable goals for others, serves to blind people to the existence of potential ethical issues (Canon, 1993); people must relearn the lesson from antiquity that the end does not justify the means.

As applied to student affairs, the work of Kitchner is most helpful (see Canon and Brown, 1985). Kitchner posits the use of five principles in the resolution of ethical and moral dilemmas: respect autonomy, do no harm, help others, be just, and be trustworthy (Canon, 1993). According to Kitchner, these principles frequently come into conflict with one another in real-life situations; therefore, the SSAO must work very hard with others to ensure that the principles are followed. In the practice of student affairs, this approach is particularly important because of the primary relationship between the SSAO and SGLs.

Whether large or small, public or private, institutional governance structures are always complex. In great part, this complexity can be traced to the fact that campus governance differs considerably from corporate, business, industrial, and government institutions. Governance in higher education is an "interactive process of achieving consensus between the governed and those governing . . . with respect to establishing mission, purpose, agenda, planning, and aspirations. In virtually no other organizational setting are there so many competing ideals, goals, and purposes as on a college and university campus" (Pembroke, 1993, p. 16). The history of American higher education has shown that the United States provides more institutional variability and curriculum alternatives than any other place in the world and that "underpinning the entire enterprise is a system of governance that in the final analysis works and works quite well" (Pembroke, 1993, p. 17).

Within this milieu, the SSAO has a duty and responsibility to coordinate the activities, functions, and responsibilities of student affairs with the mission of the institution in accordance with the governance structure, including, but not limited to, the board of trustees; standing, select, advisory, and ad hoc committees; faculty senate; staff senate; collective bargaining units; and the student governing association. Although the size, pattern, and level of involvement of the student government association (SGA) will vary from campus to campus, the relationship with the SGA must be high on the SSAO's duty list because in most cases he or she is viewed as the only institutional officer with direct responsibility for the SGA.

On most campuses, the events of the 1960s moved SGAs from the margins during an era of "limited" governance into the mainstream of shared campus governance. When one thinks of SGAs, two main images come to mind: politics and power. In regard to politics, Moore (1993, p. 152) stated that "in organizational life, the term politics may be the most employed and least understood concept among those we use to describe important aspects of our work. . . . For many faculty members and administrators, it has negative connotations, suggesting trickery, manipulation, and self-interest" (p. 152). However, Appleton stated that "political behavior is inevitable in every organizational setting, is found in every level in the hierarchy, and intensifies as the decision-making possibilities are greater and more important" (Moore, 1993, p. 152). According to Birnbaum, power may be defined as "the ability to produce intended change in others, to influence them so that they will be more likely to act in accordance with one's own preferences" (Moore, 1993, p. 152). Because of the reality of politics and power, the SSAO must combine these dynamics for constructive change.

The SSAO can learn much from the research of Kuh (1993), because he found that what and how much a student learns is primarily a function of what the student does in college, as opposed to institutional features such as size, structure, or setting. Their four essential findings are that, "first, students benefit more from their college experience when their total level of campus engagement [academic, interpersonal, and extracurricular] is mutually supporting and relevant to a particular educational outcome (Pascarella and Terenzini, 1991, p. 626). Secondly, involvement in academic and social life of the institution enhances student learning. Third, integrated and complementary academic and social programs, policies, and practices increase learning. Fourth, students who feel that they belong and are valued as individuals are more likely to take advantage of institutional resources, resulting in improved learning" (Kuh, 1993, pp. 31–32).

These four findings, combined with an understanding of politics and power, can provide a formidable and fundamental basis for an ethic of care and connectedness of students to the institution in general and elected SGA officers in particular. Thus, when we realize that politics, power, and personal development are all principles with which the SSAO must work on behalf of the students, the SSAO's commitment to these principles becomes very important to the operational mobility of the campus.

Code of Ethics

The most common structure of student government is an elected executive body, senate or assembly, and judicial branch. For the most part, highly committed students who are involved in a learning experience participate in student governments. They frequently succeed and sometimes fail, but they are first and foremost students who are involved in and care deeply about their institutions (Woodard and van Destinon, 1993).

When dealing with the SGA, it is important, if not imperative, for the SSAO to keep the following thoughts in mind and to make them part of a code of ethics. First, ethics are essential. Ethical decisions require thorough involvement and commitment. Ethical practice is not a spectator sport; the SSAO must get involved, put his or her values on the line, and match these values against the deeds of individuals and institutions with which one may not agree. It also is important to realize that ethical agendas and dilemmas are frequently determined by events quite beyond one's control (Canon, 1993).

Second, integrity is essential. The SSAO must maintain his or her integrity at all times. A person cannot cross over and expect to come back because students of all ages and backgrounds expect the SSAO to demonstrate integrity at all times and under all circumstances. There is no off switch in this domain. Integrity requires constant vigilance, and it is demanding and at times tiring, and an absolute necessity. According to Moore (1993), the gift most beneficial to the SGA is consistent ethical behavior.

Third, honesty is essential. Although institutions of higher education proclaim that they are dedicated to the pursuit of truth, observations of campus activities and decisions may lead the SSAO to a different conclusion. In dealings with the SGA, student affairs officers must be absolutely honest (Canon, 1993). The SSAO must strive to establish confidence and trust with the SGA; according to Sandeen (1991), the one principle, above all, that enables this to happen is to always be honest with the SGA. Moreover, Sandeen (1991) asserted that just one indication or perception of a lapse or an actual failure to be ethical and honest can destroy years of effort to establish and maintain trust.

Fourth, commitment is essential. The time pressures, issues, needs, concerns, and demands that confront the SSAO are incessant. Because of the vast scope and intensity of these matters, the SSAO must have voice, vision, vitality, and values. The SSAO must expect to be misinterpreted and to take considerable heat from others (Sandeen, 1993). The SSAO must maintain his or her commitment to students in a composed and confident manner.

Fifth, an ethic of care is essential. The underlying philosophy of ethics, integrity, honesty, and commitment is an ethic of care. A sense of perspective, an understanding of fairness and the common good, versatility, a sense of adventure, a commitment to community, and a generative spirit together represent commitment to an ethic of care. Canon and Brown (1985) and Gilligan (1982) have characterized this concern for relationships as a higher-order skill. When an ethic of care is present, "one invests his/her time, talents and treasures . . . to develop a special kind of student . . . who thinks logically, writes clearly, speaks truthfully, decides ethically, functions effectively, and exercises a keenly sensitive social conscience" (Clement and Rickard, 1992, p. 204).

Summary

SSAOs are responsible for people, programs, policies, procedures, finances, facilities, and services. They are frequently judged on their ability to lead, inspire, decide, serve, exercise fiscal management, improve diversity, and so on. Therefore, the SSAO, especially in dealing with the SGA, must be an effective, efficient, and ethical educator. The SSAO must actively engage the SGA and, in turn, the various constituencies associated with the SGA. The bedrock of the relationship between the SSAO and the SGA is ethical leadership; virtually everything else rests on this foundation (Sandeen, 1993). When we reflect on the questions "Why me?" "How did I get here?" "What am I doing?" and "For whom am I doing it?" the core answers are that students are essentially the reason why we go into the student affairs profession (Barr, 1993), and they are the most important reason why we stay in the profession.

Thus, we have the opportunity to serve, to challenge ourselves, to encounter the real world of decision making in the academic environment, to posit the reality of shared governance with the SGA, and to give the very best of ourselves in a selfless and ethical manner. The college experience comes and goes. The ethical lessons sustain us and serve as a framework for good for a lifetime.

References

Barr, M. J. "Becoming Successful Student Affairs Administrators." In M. J. Barr and Associates, *The Handbook of Student Affairs Administration*. San Francisco: Jossey-Bass, 1993.

Bolman, L. G., and Deal, T. E. *Reframing Organizations: Artistry, Choice, and Leadership.* San Francisco: Jossey-Bass, 1991.

Canon, H. J. "Maintaining High Ethical Standards." In M. J. Barr and Associates, *The Handbook of Student Affairs Administration*. San Francisco: Jossey-Bass, 1993.

Canon, H. J., and Brown, R. D. "How to Think About Professional Ethics." In H. J. Canon and R. D. Brown (eds.), *Applied Ethics in Student Services*. New Directions for Student Services, no. 30. San Francisco: Jossey-Bass, 1985.

Carnegie Foundation for the Advancement of Teaching. *Campus Life: In Search of Community*. Princeton, N.J.: Princeton University Press, 1990.

Clement, L. M., and Rickard, S. T. *Effective Leadership in Student Services: Voices from the Field.* San Francisco: Jossey-Bass, 1992.

Gilligan, C. *In a Different Voice: Psychological Theory and Women's Development.* Cambridge, Mass.: Harvard University Press, 1982.

Hesburgh, T. M., and Reedy, J. *God, Country, Notre Dame.* New York: Doubleday, 1990.

Horowitz, H. L. *Campus Life: Undergraduate Cultures from the End of the Eighteenth Century to the Present.* Chicago: University of Chicago Press, 1987.

Kuh, G. D. "Assessing Campus Environments." In M. J. Barr and Associates, *The Handbook of Student Affairs Administration*. San Francisco: Jossey-Bass, 1993.

Kuh, G. D., Schuh, J. H., Whitt, E. J., and Associates. *Involving Colleges: Successful Approaches* to *Fostering Student Learning and Development Outside the Classroom*. San Francisco: Jossey-Bass, 1991.

McGrath, E. J. *Should Students Share the Power?: A Study of Their Role in College and University Governance*. Philadelphia: Temple University Press, 1970.

Moore, P. L. "The Political Dimension of Decision Making." In M. J. Barr and Associates, *The Handbook of Student Affairs Administration*. San Francisco: Jossey-Bass, 1993.

Morse, S. W. *Renewing Civic Capacity: Preparing College Students for Service and Citizenship*. Washington, D.C.: George Washington University Press, 1989.

Pascarella, E. T., and Terenzini, P. T. *How College Affects Students: Findings and Insights from Twenty Years of Research*. San Francisco: Jossey-Bass, 1991.

Pembroke, W. J. "Institutional Governance and the Role of Student Affairs." In M. J. Barr and Associates, *The Handbook of Student Affairs Administration*. San Francisco: Jossey-Bass, 1993.

Sandeen, A. *The Chief Student Affairs Officer: Leader, Manager, Mediator, Educator*. San Francisco: Jossey-Bass, 1991.

Sandeen, A. "Developing Effective Campus and Community Relationships." In M. J. Barr and Associates, *The Handbook of Student Affairs Administration*. San Francisco: Jossey-Bass, 1993.

Schwartz, H. L. "An Interview Study of Former Student Leaders' Perceptions of an Ethical Conflict Involving the College or University President." *Journal of College Student Development*, 1991, *32*, 447–454.

Smith, R. N. *The Harvard Century: The Making of a University to a Nation*. New York: Simon & Schuster, 1986.

Tarbell, D.A.W. *The Story of Carnegie Tech: Being a History of Carnegie Institute of Technology from 1900 to 1935*. Pittsburgh, Pa.: Carnegie Institute of Technology, 1937.

Woodard, D. B., and van Destinon, M. "Identifying and Working with Key Constituent Groups." In M. J. Barr and Associates, *The Handbook of Student Affairs Administration*. San Francisco: Jossey-Bass, 1993.

DENNIS C. GOLDEN *is vice president for student affairs at the University of Louisville, Louisville, Kentucky, and has twenty-five years' experience as a dean of students and vice president for student affairs.*

HARRIET L. SCHWARTZ *is assistant to the dean of student affairs at Carnegie-Mellon University, Pittsburgh, Pennsylvania.*

Student affairs staff will be interested in transformational leadership principles in order to actualize their own leadership potential and to model appropriate leadership characteristics for student government leaders.

Student Government: A Testing Ground for Transformational Leadership Principles

James A. Gold, Thomas J. Quatroche

Transformational leaders do make a difference. When working with student government leaders, we are interested in both leadership and followership. One cannot leave followers out of the leadership equation, or what can be described as the expectations and constraints imposed by followers. Followers are rarely passive participants in the reality of student organizational life, perhaps even more so because of the transient and egalitarian nature of the student body governance structure. A student follower one day becomes a student leader the next day, and sometimes this happens with disarming expeditiousness. In this chapter, the focus is on training both student leaders and followers in transformational leadership principles.

The literature in the field of college student personnel, with few exceptions (Komives, 1991a, 1991b; Roueche, Baker, and Rose, 1989), has been absent references to the highly humanistic and powerfully effective transformational leadership principles espoused by Bass (1985) and others. It nevertheless appears that everyone is able to describe at least one transformational leader they have known. "He/she makes me go beyond my self-interests for the good of the group" (Bass, 1985, p. 199) is a statement that often describes the transformational leader. In contrast, "He/she makes me concentrate on my self-interests rather than what is good for the group" (p. 199) describes the transactional leader.

This chapter reviews the extensive and growing literature and research on transformational leadership, focusing on principles that may have demonstrated efficacy for successful student government management and governance in higher education. Several studies (Bass and Avolio, 1990a, 1990b,

1990c) have demonstrated the efficacy of training to improve transformational leadership ratings. A student leadership curriculum along with specific learning goals and teaching strategies should consist of transformational leadership principles as a means to create collegial governance that is inclusive, energizing, and ethically superior.

The four transformational factors that Bass and Avolio (1993, pp. 51–52) described as the basis for transformational leadership are charisma (idealized influence), inspirational motivation, intellectual stimulation, and individualized consideration. The transactional factors include contingent reward and management-by-exception (p. 52). An additional nonleadership factor (laissez-faire) is used to explain the absence of leadership through inactivity (p. 53). The reader is cautioned that, historically, many writers have used the terms *transactional, transformational,* and *charismatic* interchangeably. Proactive and active transformational efforts to lead will achieve greater results when associated with the other leadership characteristics. Charismatic and transactional characteristics are, for purposes of this chapter, to be seen as subsets or essential components of transformational leadership, and never as a complete analogue for the transformational leader profile.

Since the arrival of Burns's (1978) seminal book, *Leadership,* writers have increasingly made the distinction between transformational and transactional leaders. Educators at all levels associate leader effectiveness with charisma and intellectual stimulation (Kirby, Paradise, and King, 1992). We believe that student leaders require considerable encouragement, education, and strategic tutelage if they are to actualize the transformational characteristics of personal charisma, virtue, self-awareness, and ability to motivate and merge with others. The goal is to ennoble relationships defined as mutually enhancing, respectful, and inspiring.

The history of leadership study has focused on the traits of leadership, characteristics of personality, communication style, and hierarchical positioning. The great man or woman theory is no longer attracting attention from researchers but still captivates the public and perhaps represents much thinking of the student body when electing student leaders. However, the impact of leader-follower relations is attracting more attention today as we find new ways to empower persons throughout the organization to invest in their organization, or, more typically, to identify with the leader. If followers feel understood, appreciated, and involved in the decisions made by leaders, those leaders are considered transformational. These factors of leadership have been validated across a wide variety of organizations and cultures as well as levels of management.

Student Government

Those of us who invest considerable effort in supporting student government leaders can find no solace in Downey, Bosco, and Silver's (1984) study, which compared college experiences, adult accomplishments, and employment histories of 281 former student government participants and 203 nonparticipants.

No unique long-term effects from student government participation were found. Here is a worthy challenge to our ability and desire to make a difference by creating transformational training programs.

Student affairs staff universally recognize that conflicting agendas and paradoxical situations are the norm for higher education (Pembroke, 1993, p. 17). Therefore, preparing student leaders to assume leadership roles in a turbulent, if not incomprehensible, environment calls for a curriculum of transforming leadership principles. We are reminded that the role and influence of student government bodies deserve a high place on the agenda in discussions of institutional transformation.

Student leaders are interested in tackling big social problems both on their campuses and in their communities (Wilson, 1989). Combating racism, sexism, and homophobia as well as pushing colleges and universities to recruit and retain additional minority faculty and students require leadership skills of a transformational nature. For students, old-fashioned aggressive rhetoric and activist tactics achieved mixed results in the 1960s, and the conservative climate today is even more hostile to authoritarian demagoguery by student leaders. Yet, prior to taking office, student leaders have few opportunities to practice the more sophisticated transformational leadership skills needed to lead beyond the modest transactional roles of recognizing student organizations and funding activities and services.

During the past two decades, students have appropriately been elected to sit on many institutional governance boards. In some institutions, such as our own, students are also seated with faculty in unicameral college and university senates. For certain campuses, responsible student leaders play an important role in the development of comprehensive faculty evaluation programs (Arreola, 1987). If students are to have a role in broad institutional governance matters as well as in faculty and administrator evaluation, they should be prepared to behaviorally recognize and appropriately affirm transformational leadership traits.

Training of student leaders has necessarily focused on the practical matter of keeping student leaders attentive to their fiduciary responsibilities of effectively and ethically collecting and directing the expenditure of their mandatory student activity fees (Cufaude, 1988; Barsi, Hand, and Kress, 1985). Demonstrations of proper accounting techniques, provision of a list of valued leadership traits, practice in directing meetings, guidance in applying Robert's Rules of Order, and role-play sessions in reflective listening techniques will admittedly all be of assistance to newly elected student leaders. To additionally recommend a dynamic and thorough introduction of students to transformational leadership principles is not to demean the historical approach to training student leaders; rather, it is to call into question training programs that fall short of challenging students to consider a realistic potential to substantially transform others, including themselves as learners and leaders.

Instead of episodic nuts-and-bolts training programs, a more comprehensive longitudinal approach to individual and campuswide leadership development is needed. At Wenatchee Valley College (Schoening and Keane, 1989), promising student leaders are recruited and targeted for training before they actually emerge as leaders. Included in this program are a retreat for students and faculty focusing on leadership skills while also strengthening relationships, a credit course in student government and applied leadership, an entry of student leaders into the broadened governance structure of the institution and preparation to help them make substantive contributions to committees, and a program of campus clubs and organizations in which faculty and staff actively participate.

There are also large model approaches to viewing student leadership and comprehensive training programs for student government leaders. *A Student Government Guidebook for Evergreen Valley College* (Chavez, 1985) addresses the complete training curriculum. *A Resource Manual for Designing Training Programs* (Wood, 1981) is available from the Association of College Unions-International. Another comprehensive approach to training can be found at Brigham Young University (Call, 1985), which takes an ecological approach composed of seven steps to bring about institutional change, respecting and responding to the interactive impact between student government and the larger institution: selection of values, values translated into specific goals, designs of environment to reach goals, environment fitted to participants, measured perceptions of participants, monitored participant behavior, and data on outcomes used to redesign the environment.

With other significant players in the institution playing traditional authoritarian and hierarchical leader roles, a stand-alone approach to training student leaders, while better than no training at all, would severely limit the potential to sustain transformational student leader behavior. The interactive approach to student leadership at Brigham Young University is purposely formal, inclusive, and praiseworthy for its potential to achieve congruence between student government values and the overall values of the institution. It is within this kind of ecological and interactive framework for developing student leaders that the transformational leadership curriculum can be fully actualized.

Student Leadership

The role and influence of student government bodies cannot be ignored when discussing governance (McIntire, 1989, p. 77). A commitment by student affairs to the task of developing student leaders is as old as our profession, and fortunate is the institution where student affairs staff have been eminently involved in student government leadership development. Occasionally, elected student leaders succeed to power through an election campaign based on persistent attacks against the campus administration. Since it is human for all of us to persist in behavior that is rewarded, even if not habitual, those student leaders may themselves turn out to be highly critical, controlling, and authoritarian toward other students. They may be successful for awhile if, on that campus, there is a continuing payoff for being oppositional, or if they have legitimate rather than manufactured grievances against the campus leadership.

Student government leaders essentially preside over voluntary organizations. Principal responsibilities are collection and dispersal of student fees and the somewhat perfunctory role of recognizing student organizations. A student government president can be strengthened by transformational leadership qualities because of the lack of any permanent bureaucracy from which to provide predictable contingent reinforcements for followership loyalty and participation. The student body president needs to use his or her personality, enthusiasm, and visionary perspective to excite student senators to attend weekly meetings, which often last into the wee hours of the morning. Transformational leaders combine attractive personalities with interesting ideas. They inspire student senators to participate in time-consuming committee assignments that compete with temptations to socialize or to work for income.

Chemers (1993, p. 303) asserted that student leaders whose orientation matches the task environment have more positive moods, give higher assessments of their influence, and perceive more harmonious relationships among group members. The most important characteristics appear to be the degree of clarity, structure, and information about the task or decision and the amount of follower support. The student government leader who is trusted and inspires admiration, respect, affection, and fierce loyalty in his or her followers will have a successful year in office. On the other hand, a transactionally oriented student leader who exclusively seeks to direct, control, and bureaucratically manage resources will have reduced influence. The net result will be scattered efforts among followers, who will primarily seek individual goals that may or may not support the functions of the larger student government.

Helping student leaders to discern real problems and to ethically construct meaningful strategies toward solving them is not to meddle but rather to appropriately discharge our responsibilities as student development educators. The ability to address authentic student needs and to offer authentic relationships that respect one's constituency is the hallmark of the transformational student government leader. The credibility of student government rests on successive generations of student leaders working within an ethical framework consonant with universal standards of human rights and dignity.

Transformational Leadership

Burns (1978) articulated the concept of the transformational leader, also focusing on the changed behavior and perspective of the followers. Bass (1985) put this concept of transformational leadership into an organizational context in his seminal work on leadership performance. His book builds directly on the earlier work of Burns, providing a behavioral look at the antecedents and impact of transformational leadership from the perspective of followers. Bass's important work in transformational leadership has stimulated a plethora of applications of transformational leadership principles (sometimes described as charismatic leader characteristics).

Charismatic Leadership. The notion of the charismatic leader is an extension of the great man or woman concept because the emphasis is on the leader-follower relationship. Charismatic leaders are seen as ultimately transforming in the ways in which they influence the individual as well as the organization. How charismatic leaders develop has fascinated leaders as well as researchers (Conger, Kanungo, and Associates, 1988). Charismatic leaders are noticed for their presence, powerful influence, and compelling vision. They are often revered if not loved by their followers. Charismatic leaders strengthen the self-concepts of their followers, commanding respect and confidence, beyond what other leaders might deserve who work conscientiously but do not create emotional attachments, and imbuing their followers with transcendent goals.

Followers take on the positive traits, values, aspirations, and even mannerisms of the admired leader. Charismatic leaders deal with their inner conflicts and ambitions by throwing themselves into organizational or political life. While charismatic leaders can be expected to be charismatic in similar situations, it does not follow that the charisma is transferable to all situations. Since charismatic leaders must have a passion for the ideological goals they set forth, it is most likely that they are nonadaptable with respect to changes in the visions or the values underlying those goals (House and Shamir, 1993, p. 102).

Charisma involves an affective charge and identification with the leader that is so overwhelming that ideas about and feelings toward the leader can move beyond the conscious awareness of followers. We talk about charismatic leaders with reverence and awe, which can in some instances take on a blind quality of obedience. Such leaders embody our fantasies, dreams, and personal wish fulfillments. We project onto the leader the finest traits that are within ourselves in the hope of reaching our highest levels of ambition and satisfaction. If we idolize our leader, we somehow become ideal selves.

There are circumstances that conspire to allow us, as followers, to anoint our leader with charismatic characteristics, where the need for leadership is so glaring as to make its absence a personal organizational tragedy. There are times when student government leaders will emerge out of the chaos of misplaced or unfounded student suspicion, fear, and resentment of the campus administration or even the campus faculty.

Many student leaders do rise to power on their charismatic skills rather than management or transactional leadership skills. The ultimate success of the charismatic student leader of course depends on his or her attention to management issues, including the willingness to initiate and sustain organizational structure, rituals, and traditions. Charismatic student leaders may be successful in developing innovations, but the task of sustaining positive accomplishments requires a bureaucratic emphasis that charismatic leaders may be unwilling or unable to direct.

Like the transformational leader who may lead followers astray, benign charisma by mercurial student leaders is never guaranteed, and it is a wise student affairs staff that attempts to address student grievances proactively over time. There is the realistic hope that the college or university will be safeguarded from an overly reactionary student government if the institution is basically experienced by students as a good and respectful place to learn, grow, and interact.

Bass's (1985, pp. 201–206) Leadership Questionnaire (LQ) consists of eighty-four items. The LQ illustrates the component concepts of effective transformational and transactional leadership. The slightly revised Multifactor Leadership Questionnaire is also available (Bass and Avolio, 1990b). Each of the items of the original LQ are arranged as principal components of a five-factor structure consisting of charismatic leadership (accounted for 89.5 percent of variance of consequence), contingent reward, individualized consideration, management-by-exception, and intellectual stimulation.

In order to behaviorally translate leadership concepts into a curriculum for training student leaders, items are presented in order of weighted importance (Bass, 1985, pp. 210–212). More items are included under charismatic leadership because so much of what differentiates (89.5 percent variance) transformational leaders is found in this factor of charisma. For this reason, the following item statements from Bass's LQ are listed in priority order: "Makes everyone around him/her enthusiastic about assignments," "I have complete faith in him/her," "Is a model for me to follow," "Makes me feel good to be around him/her," "Commands respect from everyone," "Makes me proud to be associated with him/her," "I am ready to trust his/her capacity to overcome any obstacles," "Encourages me to express my ideas and opinions," "Has a special gift of seeing what it is that is really important for me to consider," "In my mind, he/she is a symbol of success and accomplishment," "Has a sense of mission which he/she transmits to me."

All of the above item statements responded to by followers are more highly factored (associated) directly with transformational leadership than are the important additional categories of inspirational motivation, intellectual stimulation, and individualized consideration. This demonstrates the powerful influence that followers attribute to charisma when defining leaders who have been transforming in their lives.

Inspirational Motivation. While inspirational leadership is most highly correlated with charismatic leadership, according to Bass (1985, p. 62) inspiration does not have to stem from charisma. Arousal of enthusiasm and strong identification with a leader's goals inspire loyalty and staunchness of purpose. Inspiration always has an emotional component, which is different from intellectual stimulation; the latter involves a separate process that supports logical rationality without regard to feelings or emotions. Inspiration by emotional appeal is a component of charismatic leadership but is not a central aspect. The use of symbols and images to focus follower efforts does appeal to strong human emotions, which may be unconscious. Item statements (Bass, 1985, p. 214) on the LQ include the following: "Is an inspiration to us," "Inspires loyalty to him/her," "Inspires loyalty to the organization."

Inspirational leadership may actually be held in disrespect by rationally oriented campus administrators and faculty leaders. But students, along with the masses in general, are often more influenced by the manipulation and demagoguery of a leader who uses persuasive appeals rather than logic. These same skills of directing follower excitement are played out at pep rallies for the football team, marches for the poor or disenfranchised, or calls for the resignation of the dean of students.

The political arousal of students, who for so many years have been the recipients of parental education and authoritarian schooling, is very difficult. It often takes a charismatic leader to excite them to action. Student leaders during the 1960s were much more willing to arouse and capable of arousing their followers to extra efforts, to propel them to higher levels of self-confidence and belief in the cause. Student leaders simply made an activist commitment to themselves, other students, and the community as a whole.

Intellectual Stimulation. Intellectual stimulation by the leader means arousal and change in followers' ways of thinking, valuing, and imagining, including how they might approach problems. Follower action does not necessarily result from such changes and new ways of solving problems. Followers are simply able to conceptualize and comprehend the challenges placed before them. Leaders must be capable of strategic planning, whereby they discern and articulate the issues facing an organization. On this basis, they conceptualize a plan of action. Such capacity to comprehend is necessary to transform the organization and the people who will deliver results. Nonintellectual student leaders may still be effective if they attract to themselves followers possessing strong intellectual and technical competence. Item statements (Bass, 1985, p. 212) on the LQ include the following: "His/her ideas have forced me to rethink some of my own ideas which I had never questioned before," "Enables me to think about old problems in new ways," "Has provided me with new ways of looking at things which used to be a puzzle to me."

Individualized Consideration. Transformational leaders are considerate of their superiors. They also tend to be friendly, intimate, and natural with their followers. Followers' self-development is supported and encouraged with benevolent consideration. This process of giving support to followers is always individualized and personalized. Respect for the unique needs of a follower, including the need for appropriate criticism, is designed to recognize special talents and provide additional opportunities for growth.

Reciprocal understanding is the goal of leader-follower interactions, and great emphasis is placed on listening to the follower's needs and expectations. Mentoring and coaching are terms that followers often use to describe the process by which their transformational leaders supervise, delegate, and evaluate. Item statements (Bass, 1985, p. 211) on the LQ include the following: "Gives personal attention to members who seem neglected," "Finds out what I want and tries to help me get it," "You can count on him/her to express his/her appreciation when you do a good job."

Transactional Leadership

When the campus is politically inactive, the transactional student leader emerges, and emphasis is on maintaining the status quo. There are, of course, times when followers appreciate the traditional leader and may perform better when leaders are authoritarian, decisive, and in substantial control of all aspects of the organization. Therefore, the leadership context must continually be factored into any portrayal of the most effective leadership equation. Transformational leaders who are consistently effective also possess strong transactional leadership skills. Our contention is that transactional skills are important for effective student leadership but they are not sufficient.

Transactional leadership is appropriate, even necessary, where student government members are inexperienced or unprepared to assume their responsibilities, which is often the case with new student government leaders. Because of the transient and mercurial nature of student government membership, there may be a large number of transactional leadership functions to be discharged, including rules and policy dissemination, structured decision making, and communication responsibilities. Some of these need to be handled by student affairs staff, perhaps in consultation with professionals employed by student government, such as a secretary and business manager. Provision of these routine administrative services and linkages is essential in order to ensure that matters of institutional ability and fiduciary (especially student activity fee disbursement) practices are appropriately and legally directed.

Because many perfunctory administrative duties are attended to by student affairs staff, the elected student government leadership is actually enabled to focus on higher-order and, therefore, potentially transforming leadership goals. This is a mixed blessing since the campus president is watchful of the student affairs staff's ability to supervise the responsibilities of student leaders while enabling those leaders to simultaneously assert the social issues of the day, which may include challenges to the policies, practices, and actions of the campus administration. Of course, some student affairs staff elect to retreat from significant involvement with student government leaders who are especially abusive and confrontational toward them, only to later regret the abandonment of their student development responsibilities.

Bass (1985, p. 176) speculated that transformational leaders are higher in social boldness, introspection, thoughtfulness, and general energy. While the transactional leader typically is higher in sociability, cooperativeness, and friendliness, the transformational leader is less conforming and finds greater satisfaction in power than does the transactional leader, who is more affiliative.

This contrast in leadership styles presents an ethical dilemma for student affairs staff. How strong do we really want our student leaders to be? Is it easier for us, and simultaneously less disconcerting, to focus all of our leadership training efforts on the safer and more delimited transactional leadership dimension? After all, there is a shadow side to transformational leadership. Transformational leaders do transform for the bad as well as the good. It is therefore incumbent on student affairs staff who train for transformational leadership to also recognize the darker side of the student leader. There is always the potential to use personal charisma and magnetism to manipulate and destroy, to exploit, seduce, and bind others as unwitting participants in a student government expedition of folly. Can we expect student government leaders to defer to the parental archetype of the campus administrator? They might bend transformational rules rather than execute their leadership roles according to ethical rules laid down by elders.

Student government provides a unique environment where transformational leadership can exist and thrive in the middle of an institution otherwise beset by a framework of highly procedural and bureaucratic transactions. No wonder student affairs staff enjoy the fray of an enthusiastic student senate debate in contrast to sitting through typically predictable administrative committee meetings. The energized, risk-taking, and intensely emotional idealism of student leaders provides a welcome contrast to the more security-oriented and status quo perspective of the professional campus leadership.

Contingent Reward. Transactional leaders place greater emphasis on contingent rewards than do transformational leaders. If people feel that their work will be acknowledged and rewarded according to a general prior agreement with a supervisor, we are observing contingent reward. Similarly, if the worker fails to deliver on the understood assignments, it is fair to expect punishment, loss of income, or negative employment appraisal. Approval is contingent on fulfillment of the leader's expectations, a simple exchange of services for an agreed-on reward. Student government leaders offer rewards that are seldom monetary but have equally important personal value, such as favored committee assignments, positive student press, faculty and administrative recognition, or special prizes and fringe benefits.

Feedback on performance is essential when people are doing the work correctly, and especially when they are not. The power to reward is cardinal to either a transactional or a transformational leader. There is no substitute for concrete feedback provided on a regular basis, enabling the follower to measure progress. Assistance in finding successful paths to goal achievement should be offered to the follower concurrently with the reward process. Item statements (Bass, 1985, pp. 210–211) from the LQ include the following: "Tells me what to do if I want to be rewarded for my efforts," "There is close agreement between what I am expected to put into the group effort and what I can get out of it," "Gives what I want in exchange for showing my support for him/her."

Management-by-Exception. Management-by-exception is sometimes a favored technique of transactional leaders who attend to management details by focusing on what is not working or what is unanticipated. Item statements (Bass, 1985, p. 212) from the LQ include the following: "As long as the old ways work, he/she is satisfied with my performance," "He/she is content to let me continue doing my job in the same way as always," "As long as things are going all right, he/she does not try to change anything."

Inexperienced student leaders often decide to rule only when things go wrong. At that point, they tend to overload followers with negative criticism where no relationship of support exists to buffer the disapprovals, reprimands, and blame by the superior. Disappointed followers then scurry to form alliances resistant to the leader or escape criticism by wholly abandoning membership in student government. The constant turnover in student government has often been attributed to competing demands for student time instead of the actual reason: poor communication by the leadership. The student government is thus thrown into crisis with fractionalized politics, which sets the tone for confrontational communication and problem solving. This neglectful form of leadership should not be confused with delegation, which is used to build confidence and increase the motivation of followers. Effective leaders who delegate responsibility are always focused on the follow-up activities of supervision and support.

Followers

The transformational leader is immoral when followers' needs are not taken into account and ethical principles that should underpin relations with persons inside and outside the organization are ignored. Student leaders who rail against fictional antagonists, whether students, administrators, faculty, or groups outside the institution, are guilty of stereotyping and appealing to base fears in their followers. This is not moral leadership. Such oversimplification of problems, attributions to imagined enemies, and assertions about conspiracies doom these student leaders to failure.

The transformational leader tends to be adaptive and resourceful in responding to different followers. It is certain that motivational leadership styles that are considerate of individuals achieve more heightened performance outcomes than do less flexible leadership styles. Relationships between and among leaders and followers dictate a contextual leadership style responsive to particular job assignments and contingencies of the moment. Leadership styles will be modified through constant feedback, including structured counseling sessions designed to achieve mutual understanding between leaders and followers. Also, transformational leaders have a knack for developing leaders from among their followers.

Negative criticism of followers is generally ineffective unless preceded by heavy doses of positive reassurance and a conviction that the follower has the ability to succeed. It also helps if the criticism is situationally directed and based on observed behavior, not on hearsay evidence. Measured criticism designed, ultimately, to enhance performance and presented in a manner designed to protect self-esteem strengthens rather than undermines the leader-follower relationship. The best-intentioned criticism, if not carefully phrased, can cause followers unnecessary anxiety, guilt, and inhibition.

Follower involvement is a key to transformational leadership effectiveness. Those who participate in the setting of work goals, the development of measures for progress, and communication about job matters are more invested in leader-follower success. New methods of self-directed and student-centered teaching techniques have parallels in good management practices. Authentic praise combined with follower involvement in goal setting and standards of evaluation provides a potent formula for motivating followers.

Implications for Practice

Effective student government leaders must be clear about the kinds of follower behavior they expect as well as what the followers will receive for delivering results. Leader behavior that inspires even higher levels of follower commitment and pursuit of leader goals is known as transformational leadership. Too often student leaders emulate the common transactional characteristics of management by control, domination, and manipulation of rewards.

A special challenge exists for student affairs staff, who are in a uniquely close association with student leaders and are capable of modeling as well as teaching transformational leadership principles and practices. As followers prove their competence and loyalty, the transformational leader affirms their status as human beings. Students, whether leaders or followers, then find that their self-interest is in accord with student government goals.

Transformational leadership, as one of the newest models of leadership, has generated a number of controversies and misconceptions about its principles, practices, and measurement (Chemers and Ayman, 1993). This leadership style, which goes beyond transactions, introduces complex variables that in some cases appear to defy measurement, presenting quantitative and qualitative assessment challenges that will be debated for some time. Yet, interest in this model has continued to boom, and student affairs staff need to test their own assumptions, values, and biases concerning leadership against the transformational model.

References

Arreola, R. A. "The Role of Student Government in Faculty Evaluation." In L. M. Aleamoni (ed.), *Techniques for Evaluating and Improving Instruction*. New Directions for Teaching and Learning, no. 31. San Francisco: Jossey-Bass, 1987.

Barsi, L. M., Hand, B., and Kress, J. L. "Training Effective Student Leaders: Back to the Basics." *NASPA Journal*, 1985, 22 (4), 26–30.

Bass, B. M. *Leadership and Performance Beyond Expectations*. New York: Free Press, 1985.

Bass, B. M., and Avolio, B. J. "The Implications of Transactional and Transformational Leadership for Individual, Team, and Organizational Development." In R. W. Woodman and W. A. Passmore (eds.), *Research in Organizational Change and Development*. Greenwich, Conn.: JAI Press, 1990a.

Bass, B. M., and Avolio, B. J. *Manual for the Multifactor Leadership Questionnaire*. Palo Alto, Calif.: Consulting Psychologist Press, 1990b.

Bass, B. M., and Avolio, B. J. "Training and Development of Transformational Leadership: Looking to 1992 and Beyond." *European Journal of Industrial Training*, 1990c, 14, 21–27.

Bass, B. M., and Avolio, B. J. "Transformational Leadership: A Response to Critiques." In M.

M. Chemers and R. Ayman (eds.), *Leadership Theory and Research*. San Diego: Academic Press, 1993.

Burns, J. M. *Leadership*. New York: HarperCollins, 1978.

Call, J. "Ecological Responses to Changing Needs of Student Government." Paper presented at the annual meeting of the National Association of Student Personnel Administrators, Portland, Oregon, Mar.-Apr. 1985.

Chavez, M. *A Student Government Guidebook for Evergreen Valley College*. San Jose, Calif.: Evergreen Valley College, 1985.

Chemers, M. M. "An Integrative Theory of Leadership." In M. M. Chemers and R. Ayman (eds.), *Leadership Theory and Research*. San Diego: Academic Press, 1993.

Chemers, M. M., and R. Ayman (eds.). *Leadership Theory and Research*. San Diego: Academic Press, 1993.

Conger, J. A., Kanungo, R. N., and Associates. *Charismatic Leadership: The Elusive Factor in Organizational Effectiveness*. San Francisco: Jossey-Bass, 1988.

Cufaude, J. "Back to Basics: Training Student Funding Boards." *Campus Activities Programming*, 1988, *20* (9), 52–56.

Downey, R. G., Bosco, P. J., and Silver, E. M. "Long-Term Outcomes of Participation in Student Government." *Journal of College Student Personnel*, 1984, *25* (3), 245–250.

House, R. J., and Shamir, B. "Toward the Integration of Transformational, Charismatic, and Visionary Theories." In M. M. Chemers and R. Ayman (eds.), *Leadership Theory and Research*. San Diego: Academic Press, 1993.

Kirby, P. C., Paradise, L. V., and King, M. I. "Extraordinary Leaders in Education: Understanding Transformational Leadership." *Journal of Educational Research*, 1992, *85* (5), 303–311.

Komives, S. R. "Gender Differences in the Relationship of Hall Directors' Transformational and Transactional Leadership Styles." *Journal of College Student Development*, 1991a, *32* (2), 155–165.

Komives, S. R. "The Relationship of Hall Directors' Transformational and Transactional Leadership to Select Resident Assistant Outcomes." *Journal of College Student Development*, 1991b, *32* (6), 509–515.

McIntire, D. D. "Student Leadership Development: A Student Affairs Mandate." *NASPA Journal*, 1989, *27* (1), 75–79.

Pembroke, W. J. "Institutional Governance and the Role of Student Affairs." In M. J. Barr and Associates, *The Handbook of Student Affairs Administration*. San Francisco: Jossey-Bass, 1993.

Roueche, J. E., Baker, G. A., III, and Rose, R. R. *Shared Vision: Transformational Leadership in American Community Colleges*. Alexandria, Va.: American Association of Community and Junior Colleges, 1989.

Schoening, D., and Keane, C. "Student Success Through Leadership." Paper presented at the Student Success Strategies Conference, Portland, Oregon, Feb. 1989.

Wilson, R. "Student Leaders from Big Ten Campuses Organize to Revitalize Activism." *Chronicle of Higher Education*, Sept. 20, 1989, pp. A40–A41.

Wood, S. A. *A Resource Manual for Designing Training Programs*. Stanford, Calif.: Association of College Unions-International, 1981.

JAMES A. GOLD is associate professor of the Educational Foundations Department, SUNY College, Buffalo.

THOMAS J. QUATROCHE is chair of the Educational Foundations Department and coordinator of the student personnel administration program, SUNY College, Buffalo.

With observed and predicted growth in social and political activism among students, higher education and community leaders are challenged to rethink the impact of student activism on students' development and on institutional and community change processes.

Student Activism: Impacting Personal, Institutional, and Community Change

Tony Chambers, Christine E. Phelps

> We are people of this generation, bred in at least modest comfort, housed now in universities, looking uncomfortably to the world we inherit.
>
> —J. Miller (1987, p. 329)

College student activism influences change beyond the students themselves and the education institution in which they are a part. Student activism is neither place-bound (specific to a particular global region, institutional type, or type of individual) nor issue-bound (specific to a particular issue or category of issues). The dynamic nature of college student activism supports and ensures a consistency of presence on college campuses around the world. The degree and intensity to which that consistency of presence exists at any given time and in any given environmental context reflect the rapidly changing times and circumstances in particular environments and among students. The realities of racial, gender, affectional, and cultural injustices; institutional decisions that differentially and negatively impact students; environmental issues; war; economic stresses and uncertainties; and questionable leadership at home and abroad have all sparred with the youthful idealism and optimism of college students to provide a consistency of presence of campus activism. This ebb and flow of activist engagement has had both direct and indirect impacts on the ways in which higher education institutions have evolved their governance structures. As well, the significant impact of college student activism has been felt by the environments and communities beyond the campuses.

   Activism, within the context of this chapter, is defined as the active participation of individuals in group behavior, for the purpose of creating change—

in attitudes, knowledge, behavior, and symbols (Chambers and Phelps, 1991). The expected change can be directed toward individuals, groups, or systems. Based on this definition, we conclude that all student activism is student leadership. Further, we strongly believe that the focus on change among college student activists juxtaposes the purposes and operations of institutional governance, community and social involvement, and student activist engagement. And, as such, the frameworks available for thinking about student leadership, community service, and participation in institutional governance are appropriately viewed and understood within the context of student activism.

Further, we recognize that there are acts of social and political engagement that have as their primary purpose nonproductive destruction and disruption. However, our discussion speaks to those activist behaviors directed toward the creation of change to address perceived or real inequities between and among individuals, groups, or systems.

The purpose of this chapter is to discuss the impact of student activism on campus and community governance and on individual student leadership abilities. The central beliefs of the chapter are that college student activism significantly influences the development of leadership abilities among those who engage in such activities and that college student activism significantly impacts the ways in which higher education institutions are governed. Additionally, we believe that student activism and community involvement share a seamless relationship in which students have, historically, exerted leadership to effect significant social change.

From these central beliefs, the following questions are explored in this chapter: How have student activists been involved in institutional governance in higher education? What is the relationship between student activism and community involvement? How does involvement in student activism influence a student's leadership development?

The final and most critical question addressed in this discourse is "So what?" In other words, what does the relationship among students, institutions, and communities mean in the context of social and political activist involvement? Why discuss these issues? What are the lessons learned and future opportunities envisioned from such lessons?

In this chapter, we, first, provide a brief history of student activism. Then we summarize some of the issues and concerns related to student activism, as well as how institutions have responded to activism. A discussion of activism as a form of leadership development follows. We conclude with a discussion of implications for educators who are interested in students' involvement in institutional and community change, as well as enhancing students' leadership capacities through social and political activism.

A Brief History of Student Activism

Throughout most of the world, and especially in Third World nations, university students are a major political force. Strikes, boycotts, riots, and picketing by students are almost commonplace and have been influential in toppling governments, forcing changes in public policy, and making or breaking political careers. Examples include the Tianamen Square student occupation in China and the major role of South Korean student activism in the dramatic changes in South Korean politics. By comparison, U.S. students have been politically passive (Miles, 1971; Choi, 1991). As in other countries, student activism has been a part of the higher education experience in the United States since the earliest colleges were established in the colonial period. Since that time, students on American campuses have made significant contributions to higher education through their organized protests, rebellion, and leadership. As the foci of protests have changed over the years, so too have institutional and community reactions.

The first recorded American student rebellion occurred at Harvard University in 1766 because of the poor quality of butter served in the Commons. Few of the protests that occurred during the nineteenth century had an ideological basis or were concerned with national politics. Rather, these early complaints were directed toward services provided, activities available, and requirements such as compulsory attendance at religious services (Brax, 1981).

Numerous student protests took place across the country between 1870 and 1900 and typically involved one of two themes: in loco parentis and the removal of unpopular college presidents. In the early nineteenth century, violence was prevalent in student protest, ranging from property destruction at Princeton University (Wertenbaker, 1946) to the death of a professor at the University of Virginia (Bruce, 1920–1922). By the close of the century, student activism had prompted the establishment of debating clubs, literary societies and magazines, fraternities, elaborate student government systems, and the sanctioning of sporting events (Ellsworth and Burns, 1970).

At the turn of the century, broader issues, particularly those of a social and political nature, began to attract the attention of students. The limited activism that existed during this time often centered around helping newly arrived immigrants and urban poor (Brax, 1981). For the first time, antiwar sentiment emerged, and from this came the formation of the Intercollegiate Socialist Society (ISS), which later became Students for a Democratic Society. This was a major development in student activism because ISS represented the first ideologically oriented national student organization in the United States (Altbach, 1974).

The 1920s brought an increase of student criticism directed toward higher education. Students charged that the curriculum was not relevant to social concerns, questioned the role of higher education, and became concerned about academic freedom. At the same time, opposition to war continued to build, resulting in the peace strikes of the 1930s. During this decade, the ramifications of the Depression and the rumblings of war produced and sustained a period of student activism of a scope and intensity previously unknown to American society (Brax, 1981). This decade saw the first nationally organized student movement in America, which provided an era of training for many of the leaders in the postwar society. New student organizations were formed, such as the American Student Union, which increased the numbers of students involved in campus unrest (Altbach, 1974).

The momentum of the student movement of the 1930s was an early casualty of World War II. General disinterest in politics was evident in the "silent generation" of the 1950s (Brax, 1981). New students on campus, including war veterans, were prone to conformity and stabilization, not activism. The conservative nature of American society and the rise of political repression were reflected in a student population uninvolved in social issues (Baxter Magolda and Magolda, 1988).

Events of the 1960s reordered the world, in particular the education community. Four themes characterize the activism of this decade: civil rights, civil liberties, the peace movement, and student life. While certain themes were prominent at different times in the 1960s, all were intertwined and had a collective impact on higher education (Baxter Magolda and Magolda, 1988). In 1969, at the height of the protest period, 28 percent of the college population had participated in a demonstration of some kind during their years in college (Levine, 1980), and the number increased to 50 percent by the spring of 1970 (Lipset, 1976).

It is important to recognize the distinctive dynamics of the African American student movement, and the overall influence that movement had on student activism during the 1960s. Young African American college students played a significant role in the black social movement, which was largely responsible for the social gains experienced by African Americans during the 1970s. While still confronting racism and other forms of discrimination in society and education, African American students forged a strategic design that other student activist leaders emulated over time, as they often appeared more organized and cohesive than their white peers (Long, 1970; Jewell, 1985). The African American student movement is similar to Third World revolutionary movements, such as those in Ghana, China, Cuba, and Algeria. These have been struggles for self-determination by people of color against white Western colonial or neocolonial domination (Miles, 1971).

Collectively, the events of the 1960s resulted in expanded student rights. These changes were evident in clearer academic procedures and expectations, a larger student role in institutional governance, and deregulation of student life. Student rights expanded as grading systems were improved, education requirements were further specified, and student input in teacher evaluation was formalized. Greater involvement in institutional governance was evident in the increasing student input in existing committees and the creation of new committees to review campus issues (Astin, Astin, Bayer, and Bisconti, 1975).

Toward the end of the 1970s, the student movement was radicalized and dissolving, and campuses began to institutionalize the movement gains of the preceding decade. Student protests had succeeded in bringing about many changes, including the end of the parietals and the beginning of student-initiated courses, policies, procedures, and personnel that responded to the concerns of African American students, as well as the beginning of the U.S. with-drawal from Vietnam. In addition, women's centers and African American stu-dent unions found permanent homes on many campuses, gay and lesbian students began to create formal organizations, and student governments con-tinued to seek a greater role in university operations (Horowitz, 1986; Long, 1970; Vellela, 1988).

The 1980s was a decade in which students were serious about profes-sional preparation. Rebellion was more quiet and assumed a new form, as stu-dent activists did not openly protest and sought separation from the grade consciousness of their careerist peers (Horowitz, 1986). The protests of this decade were considerably more reasoned and sophisticated than many of the protests of the Vietnam era, primarily because the organizers had learned from their predecessors. Some activism did occur in the mid 1980s, and the lead-ing issue was often opposition to apartheid. Students agitated on hundreds of campuses, and many were successful in forcing their universities to divest holdings in South Africa (Vellela, 1988).

Impacting the ways in which higher education institutions are governed is a major focus of contemporary campus activists. Today's student activists realize that their fees, contributions, and tax dollars support their colleges and universities. As a result, students have injected themselves into the institutional decision-making process in a number of areas: the granting of tenure to pro-fessors; creation of new classes, courses, and programs; investments in the institution's portfolio; admissions policies; grant and loan procedures; labor conditions on campus; government and corporate research contracts executed on campus; and selection of the businesses patronized by the institution in its purchase of goods and services. Students frequently serve with administrators and faculty on committees studying such issues as racial problems, recruitment of more minority faculty, and rising tuition. Student government is viewed as more of a political role than the social role that it once was. Student govern-ments increasingly view themselves as advocates for full rights for students in areas such as free speech, policy decisions, disciplinary proceedings, and the conduct of the institution's business. A voice for students in the overall deci-sion-making process is typically sought, rather than a confrontational stance (Vellela, 1988). Students today continue to protest against social issues such as racism, sexism, homophobia, divestment policies, and abortion rights. In addition, environmental concerns have moved to the forefront (Collison, 1990; Vellela, 1988).

Student Activism: Issues and Concerns

Professional literature on student leadership, institutional governance, and civic service (to a lesser degree) have traditionally focused on students involved in particular leadership roles. Programmatic efforts, institutional structures, and scholarship in these areas have dealt primarily with the behavioral and attitu-dinal changes, development, and growth of student government officers, residence hall officers, fraternity and sorority members, student paraprofessionals, and members of various student organizations that are recognized and often supported by institutions and key individuals such as alumni or trustees.

Studies of the history of leadership among students in institutions of higher education have focused, to the greatest extent, on the perspective of the "institutionally accepted organized group." Students who have been involved in social and political activism within formal educational settings either have been studied outside of the institutions' developmental milieu or else have not been studied at all. There are notable exceptions in the literature that focus on students' activism from a developmental perspective (Keniston, 1969, 1971; Katz, 1967; Katz and Associates, 1968). However, the overwhelming perspective of student activist behavior as either leadership or developmental (cognitive, psychosocial, or behavioral) is limited in the literature because activism is often seen as disruptive to the educational process rather than complementary to it (Altbach, 1989a; Altbach and Cohen, 1990; Cohen, 1985; Craig, 1984). Likewise, student activists' impact on institutional decision making has been conspicuously absent from the discussion on institutional change and governance. Student activism has been viewed by many members of the education community, as well as those outside of the community, as disorderly, rowdy, misdirected actions of less serious minded youth who place little value on education (Altbach, 1989b; Brax, 1981; Foster and Long, 1970; Horowitz, 1986)—or, as simply stated by Spiro Agnew, "an effete corps of impudent snobs." It is our position that the observed and predicted resurgence of college student activism is best viewed by education and community leaders as a form of leadership development and a critical part of a student's developmental process. The insights derived from examining student activism from a developmental perspective contribute to our knowledge about students' involvement, decision making, sense of community, and social commitment as well as provide additional perspectives on institutional and community change processes.

Sandeen (1985, p. 5) noted that much of the change in student culture, and perhaps a major influence on increased activism over the last couple of decades, has occurred primarily as a result of "the shift to more conservative attitudes in the larger society." Students reflect those values and attitudes in their personal, academic, and social choices. Examples of how these attitudes and values are exhibited in school environments include the protests and counterprotests to U.S. participation in conflicts around the world and the ongoing debates on abortion, affirmative action and racism, freedom of speech and other individual rights, and what constitutes cultural literacy.

There have been observations and predictions of increased activism among students (Altbach and Cohen, 1990; Astin, 1990; Horowitz, 1989; Levine and Hirsch, 1990; Meyer, 1985; Watkins, 1986), though the level and kind of activist behavior appear to be low key. Levine (1980) recognized three possible reasons for the low visibility of contemporary activism: First, there are multiple issues on which activism is focused; second, issues vary from institution to institution, state to state, and person to person; and, third, the approaches taken by contemporary activists tend to be peaceful and specialized in terms of the particular group.

An additional factor that contributes to the low visibility of student activism is the increase in cultural diversity among students, which, ironically, makes the development of a unified student voice more difficult, since the ethnic heritages and cultural values of students from diverse backgrounds are quite different from those of traditional students (Carter, 1990; Fleming, 1984). Also, the increase in diversity introduces other possible issues for students to champion as legitimate social concerns. On the college level, there continues to be an increase in the number of returning part-time female students, who tend to be older than traditional-age students. These women typically are commuter students, and college is not the central, or exclusive, part of their daily lives. This reduced proportion of time spent at the institutions limits the likelihood of activist involvement of a highly visible nature (Aslanian and Brickell, 1980; Evans, 1985; Frances, 1989; Hall and Sandler, 1982, 1984; Hughes, 1983; Levine, 1981).

Other concerns include the questions What factors contribute to the emergence of student activism? and How does student activism contribute to other meaningful student experiences? In a set of longitudinal studies, Astin (1990) related students' involvement and values to their degrees of commitment to participate in community service. Among the findings in these studies were that students who were involved in community service in college (1) participated in campus activism, (2) had faculty who had a high commitment to social change, (3) had a peer group who had a high commitment to social change, and (4) were social activists and volunteers in high school. Based on data collected over the prior twenty-five years on activists' involvement in high school and their expected activist involvement in college, Astin (1990, 1992) found that the rate of activism among students today is higher than what was observed in the late 1960s. The interest in influencing social values and in influencing the political structure showed sharp increases over the prior six years among incoming college freshmen (Astin, Dey, Korn, and Riggs, 1992). Along with these increased interests in social issues and political structures has been a mushrooming of college student involvement in community service activities (Levine and Hirsch, 1991). The most striking observation regarding the increase in community service among college students concerns the commitment of students to "sustained and very real and intractable social issues" (Levine and Hirsch, 1991, p. 125). The difference is that earlier community service activities by students were more short term and less focused on deep, extensive community issues.

Student activism, notwithstanding the complexities of the changing student demographics and the multiple foci of activists, has survived the test of time. The history of student activism has provided a perspective on adaptation to change and a testimony to the omnipresence of leadership through activist engagement.

Institutional Reactions to Student Activism

Traditionally, responses to student activism have been reactive rather than proactive, with a tendency to seek quick fixes rather than plan for long-term solutions (Foster and Long, 1970; Vellela, 1988). Institutional and community responses to student protest activities have varied over time according to the nature of the protest, the nature of the institution, and the relationship between the institution and its students. Historically, student protest has been met with severe responses because of the in loco parentis relationship between the institution and its students. In addition, academe was entrenched in its own methods of decision making and often reacted negatively to the suggested processes of studying issues, drawing recommendations from study groups, fully discussing recommendations in the academic community, and developing consensus among members of the academic community. Needless to say, protesters often viewed these negative reactions as avoidance and delay tactics. Given this adversarial environment, responses by institutions were often ineffective. Typical institutional response strategies were restrictive actions, attempts at persuasion, and limited concessions to demands. A review of these strategies reveals that early and continuous communication was most effective in dealing with both the activists' tactics as well as the issues on which the activism was based (Baxter Magolda and Magolda, 1988; Foster and Long, 1970). Furthermore, a preventive strategy appears to be the best policy in dealing with university protest, followed by a concessive strategy.

Current reactions to protest have a different tone. College and university administrators often attempt to use conflict management skills and are more willing to meet with students in a negotiation process before calling in the police. However, in contrast to the protests of the 1960s, student activism today is marked by civility, attributed to the fact that students today are more involved with campus decision making. Rules and policies are spelled out far in advance of protests to limit surprises and curtail possible violence.

Student Activism as Leadership Development

A central purpose of education is to prepare mature individuals for active citizenship and to assume positions of leadership (McIntire, 1989; Roberts and Ullom, 1989; Wheeler, 1985). In various ways, institutions have encouraged the development of leadership skills among students and provided opportunities for that leadership to emerge (DeJulio, Larson, Deuer, and Paulman, 1981; Roberts and Ullom, 1989; Striffolino and Saunders, 1989). Students have functioned in a variety of leadership roles, inside and outside of formal educational settings, throughout the years. They have assumed leadership roles such as resident advisers, academic aides, peer counselors, student government officers, fraternity and sorority members, officers of clubs and organizations, members of institutionwide committees, and representatives to institutional and systemwide governing bodies. Students' interests and involvement in decision making have contributed to institutional vitality and much of the change previously discussed here (Collison, 1990). Student leaders have provided an invaluable, oftentimes irreplaceable resource at many education institutions (DeJulio, Larson, Deuer, and Paulman, 1981).

Although much of the research on student leadership focuses on student involvement within educational environments, community-based organizations have contributed a considerable amount to the development of student leaders and social activists. Gardner (1987) recognized the value of community-based experiences for students: opportunities for students to test their judgment under pressure in the face of opposition, and in the fluid and swiftly changing circumstances so characteristic of action; opportunities to exercise responsibilities and perhaps to try out one or another of the skills required for leadership; opportunities for students to test and sharpen their intuitive gifts, and to judge their impact on others; exposure to new constituencies; and exposure to the untidy world, where decisions must be made with inadequate information and the soundest argument does not always win, and where problems do not get fully solved, or, if solved, surface anew in another form.

While Gardner (1987) focused primarily on the value of leadership experiences in community-based settings, this same value applies directly to activists' experiences as well. The positive and significant nature of college student activism has received considerable recognition. The U.S. President's Commission on Campus Unrest (1970) viewed student activism not as a social problem but rather as a natural consequence of renewal in the life of the mind. Flacks (1988) noted the deliberateness of student activism, where human action was seen as "directed at the making of history." Consistent with Chambers and Phelps's (1991) definition of activism, Astin, Astin, Bayer, and Bisconti (1975, p. 5) defined protest as "any organized activity involving members of the campus community and occurring on or about campus for the purpose of excessive disapproval of or to bring about change in some policy, practice, or event." Many of the same kinds of comments and perspectives have been shared regarding student leadership involvement on college campuses and in their surrounding communities.

Other student leadership studies have addressed the values of involvement and commitment to change, which are essential to activism. Results from studies on the relationship between leadership involvement and personal and social life satisfaction have been generally positive. Power-Ross (1980) found that cocurricular involvement of students has a positive effect in areas of development, such as increased cultural and social awareness and personal and social skills. Astin (1977) noted that involvement in student leadership was related to above-average increases in political liberalism, hedonism, and artistic interest. Leadership involvement had a positive influence on satisfaction with student friendships; however, it had a negative influence on satisfaction with the intellectual climate of the educational setting.

Summary and Conclusion

Although students who have engaged in political and social activist behaviors have had limited representation in the literature on student development and leadership, contemporary student development paradigms and leadership perspectives can be viewed within the context of student activism. Student activism has been around since the beginning of this country's existence. The quality and quantity of activist involvement have changed over time, depending on societal values, students' knowledge and personal commitments, institutional support or resistance, the types of causes and issues, and the demographic composition of students in particular educational environments. By the definition provided in this chapter, activism is a developmental phenomena, and the participants in activist engagement are participating in acts of leadership as well.

Recognition of student activism as a form of leadership and development and a contributor to institutional change is important for a number of reasons: (1) A refocusing of perspectives held by education and community leaders on the constructive and progressive aspects of activism, as opposed to its destructive and regressive aspects, will provide additional information about the impact of college on students, and vice versa. (2) Operational definitions of student leadership, and the premises on which leadership programs are developed, will be challenged to recognize the value of activist behavior and thought to the study and practice of leadership. And (3) future research on both leadership and student development can explore the different dynamics of development that occur among student activists.

As student activism increases in educational environments, efforts to promote and ensure the continued recognition of student activists as contributors to the educational milieu and mission will become critical. Research by leadership, student development, and institutional change scholars can contribute significantly to the literature on such issues as the moral and ethical development of student activists, the modeling behaviors of traditional student leaders and student activists, student activists' long-term commitment to social change, the effects of race and gender in the decision to engage in particular activist behaviors, the influence of institutional policies and services on the emergence of student activism, the roles of faculty, administrators, and peers in the development of student leaders and activists, and the personalities and values of student activists and student leaders. Additionally, there are policy and procedural implications accompanying the recognition of student activism's legitimacy. In addition to the many institutional and communitywide issues in which student activists are involved, other, more specific student-focused policy and procedural areas include student discipline and grievances, funding and support of student organizations, place and manner of student free speech, use of institutional facilities, full participation of students in institutional governance, access to student records by outside agents (for example, police and federal agencies), involvement of off-campus individuals in on-campus activism, and the general codes or expectations of student life.

The educational environment today provides multiple opportunities for students to become involved in their own learning and in the shaping of institutional policies, procedures, and positions on many critical issues. In addition to the increasing cultural diversity in education institutions, there are diverse degrees of commitment to social, political, and institutional causes and issues. Students who choose to act on their social and political commitments are no less a part of the education process than those students who choose to express themselves in other ways. Student activism has been, and will continue to be, an important part of students' learning experiences, whether as participants or observers. In recognizing the influence of activism on the development of students and the impact of their experiences on institutions, members of education communities can explore and learn from the actions and thoughts of involved students. In many ways, to clarify activism's legitimacy as a source of developmental and institutional change is to clarify the future of student involvement and leadership in education.

References

Altbach, P. G. *Student Politics in America: A Historical Analysis.* New York: McGraw-Hill, 1974.

Altbach, P. G. "Perspectives on Student Political Activism." *Comparative Education,* 1989a, 25 (1), 97–110.

Altbach, P. G. "Students and the Conflicts of the Sixties." *Comparative Education,* 1989b, 33 (3), 377–380.

Altbach, P. G., and Cohen, R. "American Student Activism: The Post-Sixties Transformation." *Journal of Higher Education,* 1990, 61 (1), 32–49.

Aslanian, C. B., and Brickell, H. M. *Americans in Transition: Life Changes as Reasons for Adult Learning.* New York: College Entrance Examination Board, 1980.

Astin, A. W. *Four Critical Years: Effects of College on Beliefs, Attitudes, and Knowledge.* San Francisco: Jossey-Bass, 1977.

Astin, A. W. "Institutional Commitment and Student Involvement in Community Service." Paper presented at California Campus Compact, Los Angeles, Dec. 1990.

Astin, A. W. *What Matters in College? Four Critical Years Revisited.* San Francisco: Jossey-Bass, 1992.

Astin, A. W., Astin, H. S., Bayer, A. E., and Bisconti, A. S. *The Power of Protest.* San Francisco: Jossey-Bass, 1975.

Astin, A. W., Dey, E. L., Korn, W. S., and Riggs, E. R. *The American Freshman: National Norms for Fall 1992.* Los Angeles: Higher Education Research Institute, University of California, 1992.

Baxter Magolda, M. B., and Magolda, P. M. "Student Activism: A Historical Overview." In K. M. Miser (ed.), *Student Affairs and Campus Dissent: Reflection of the Past and Challenge for the Future.* Monograph No. 8. Washington, D.C.: National Association of Student Personnel Administrators, 1988.

Brax, R. S. *The First Student Movement.* Port Washington, N.Y.: Kennikat Press, 1981.

Bruce, P. A. *History of the University of Virginia, 1819–1919.* New York: Macmillan, 1920–1922.

Carter, R. T. "Cultural Value Differences Between African Americans and White Americans." *Journal of College Student Development,* 1990, 10 (1), 71–79.

Chambers, A., and Phelps, C. "Back to the Future: Student Activism as a Form of Leadership Development." Paper presented at the annual meeting of the American College Personnel Association, Atlanta, Apr. 1991.

Choi, H. "The Societal Impact of Student Politics in Contemporary South Korea." *Higher Education,* 1991, *22,* 175–188.

Cohen, R. "Berkeley Free Speech Movement: Paving the Way for Campus Activism." *OAH Magazine of History,* 1985, *1* (1), 16–18.

Collison, M. N. "Negotiation, Not Violence Is the Rule Today When Students Clash with Administrators." *Chronicle of Higher Education,* May 2, 1990, pp. A30–A32.

Craig, S. C. "Political Discontent and Participatory Styles: An Exploratory Study of College Youths." *Youth and Society,* 1984, *15* (4), 469–493.

DeJulio, S. S., Larson, K., Deuer, E., and Paulman, R. "The Measurement of Leadership Potential in College Students." *Journal of College Student Personnel,* 1981, *22,* 207–213.

Ellsworth, F. L., and Burns, M. A. *Student Activism in Higher Education.* Monograph No. 10. Washington, D.C.: American College Personnel Association, 1970.

Evans, N. J. (ed.). *Facilitating the Development of Women.* New Directions for Student Services, no. 29. San Francisco: Jossey-Bass, 1985.

Flacks, R. *Making History: The American Left and the American Mind.* New York: Columbia University Press, 1988.

Fleming, J. *Blacks in College: A Comparative Study of Students' Success in Black and White Institutions.* San Francisco: Jossey-Bass, 1984.

Foster, J., and Long, D. (eds.). *Protest: Student Activism in America.* New York: William Morrow, 1970.

Frances, C. "Uses and Misuses of Demographic Projections: Lessons for the 1990s." In A. Levine and Associates, *Shaping Higher Education's Future.* San Francisco: Jossey-Bass, 1989.

Gardner, J. W. *Leadership Development.* Washington, D.C.: INDEPENDENT SECTOR, 1987.

Hall, R. M., and Sandler, B. R. *The Classroom Climate: A Chilly One for Women?* Washington, D.C.: Association of American Colleges, 1982.

Hall, R. M., and Sandler, B. R. *Out of the Classroom: A Chilly Climate for Women?* Washington, D.C.: Association of American Colleges, 1984.

Horowitz, H. L. "The 1960s and the Transformation of Campus Cultures." *History of Education Quarterly,* 1986, *26* (1), 1–38.

Horowitz, H. L. "The Changing Student Culture: A Retrospective." *Educational Record,* 1989, *70* (3–4), 24–29.

Hughes, R. "The Non-Traditional Student in Higher Education: A Synthesis of the Literature." *NASPA Journal,* 1983, *20* (3), 51–64.

Jewell, K. S. "Will the Real Black, Afro-American, Mixed, Colored, Negro, Please Stand Up? Impact of the Black Social Movement, Twenty Years Later." *Journal of Black Studies,* 1985, *16* (1), 57–75.

Katz, J. "The Student Activists: Rights, Needs, and Power of Student Undergraduates." In *New Dimensions in Higher Education.* Washington, D.C.: Government Printing Office, 1967.

Katz, J., and Associates. *No Time for Youth: Growth and Constraint in College Students.* San Francisco: Jossey-Bass, 1968.

Keniston, K. "Moral Development, Youth Activism, and Modern Society." *Youth and Society,* 1969, *1* (1), 110–127.

Keniston, K. *Youth and Dissent: The Rise of a New Opposition.* Orlando, Fla.: Harcourt Brace Jovanovich, 1971.

Levine, A. *When Dreams and Heroes Died: A Portrait of Today's College Student.* San Francisco: Jossey-Bass, 1980.

Levine, A. "The College Student: A Changing Constituency." In P. G. Altbach and R. O. Berdahl (eds.), *Higher Education in American Society.* Buffalo, N.Y.: Prometheus, 1981.

Levine, A., and Hirsch, D. "Student Activism and Optimism Return to the Campus." *Chronicle of Higher Education,* Nov. 7, 1990, p. A48.

Levine, A., and Hirsch, D. "Undergraduates in Transition: A New Wave of Activism on American College Campuses." *Higher Education,* 1991, *22,* 119–128.

Lipset, S. M. *Rebellion in the University.* Chicago: University of Chicago Press, 1976.

Long, D. "Black Protest." In J. Foster and D. Long (eds.), *Protest: Student Activism in America.* New York: William Morrow, 1970.

McIntire, D. D. "Student Leadership Development: A Student Affairs Mandate." *NASPA Journal,* 1989, 27 (1), 75–79.

Meyer, T. J. "Students Seen Emerging as a Political Force; Many Wonder How Long They Can Afford College." *Chronicle of Higher Education,* Sept. 4, 1985, pp. 29, 36.

Miles, M. W. *The Radical Probe: The Logic of Student Rebellion.* New York: Atheneum, 1971.

Miller, J. *Democracy in the Streets.* New York: Simon & Schuster, 1987.

Power-Ross, S. K. "Co-Curricular Activities Validated Through Research." *Student Activities Programming,* 1980, *13,* 46–48.

Roberts, D., and Ullom, C. "Student Leadership Program Model." *NASPA Journal,* 1989, 27 (1), 67–74.

Sandeen, A. "The Shift to Conservatism: Implications for Student Affairs." *NASPA Journal,* 1985, 22 (4), 2–8.

Striffolino, P., and Saunders, S. A. "Emerging Leaders: Students in Need of Development." *NASPA Journal,* 1989, 27 (1), 51–58.

U.S. President's Commission on Campus Unrest. *The Report of the President's Commission on Campus Unrest.* Washington, D.C.: Government Printing Office, 1970.

Vellela, T. *New Voices: Student Activism in the Eighties and Nineties.* Boston: South End Press, 1988.

Watkins, B. T. "Although Student Protest Is on the Rise, It's Not Like Sixties Veteran Activist Says." *Chronicle of Higher Education,* Nov. 19, 1986, pp. 35, 37.

Wertenbaker, T. J. *Princeton, 1746–1896.* Princeton, N.J.: Princeton University Press, 1946.

Wheeler, E. "Educating Leaders: When Did You Last See a Budding Thomas Jefferson on Campus?" *Chronicle of Higher Education,* Dec. 11, 1985, p. 92.

TONY CHAMBERS is assistant professor of higher education administration and student affairs at Michigan State University, East Lansing. He is also a W. K. Kellogg National Fellow and senior associate with the Heartland Center for Leadership Development.

CHRISTINE E. PHELPS is assistant professor of education in the Department of Leadership and Counseling at Eastern Michigan University, Ypsilanti. She is also a directorate member of the American College Personnel Association Commission XII (Graduate Preparation Programs in Student Personnel).

Student affairs professionals must continue to encourage ethnic minority students to become widely involved in student governance activities. This involvement will help to foster an environment that promotes human growth and development and also aid the institution in retaining these students.

Assessing Ethnic Minority Student Leadership and Involvement in Student Governance

Bruce D. Lavant, Melvin C. Terrell

As a result of the civil rights movement and other historical and egalitarian efforts that opened the doors of higher education to underrepresented populations, ethnic minority students continue to enroll in predominantly white institutions (Jones, 1987) and recruitment efforts to attract them have been accelerated. Numerous studies indicate, however, that the overall experiences of ethnic minority students attending predominantly white institutions vary from institution to institution (Fleming, 1981; Pounds, 1987; Hughes, 1987; Bourassa, 1991). Consequently, the higher education community must continue to ensure that the campus environment is perceived by all students as supportive, bias-free, and hospitable (Stennis-Williams, Terrell, and Haynes, 1988).

According to Astin (1982) and Fleming (1981, 1984), too many ethnic minority students perceive too many college or university campuses as hostile. These perceptions produce lasting negative attitudes and affect the manner in which students become involved in campus life as well as the rates of matriculation (and nonmatriculation) and retention of these special populations.

In this chapter, we describe a study that was undertaken to evaluate and determine the level at which ethnic minority students were involved in student leadership and student governance-related activities on predominantly white campuses. We also discuss the implications of our findings on minority student involvement for the collegiate experience of students of color, and we posit a framework for understanding the relationship between student involvement and institutional efforts to retain students of color.

NEW DIRECTIONS FOR STUDENT SERVICES, no. 66, Summer 1994 © Jossey-Bass Publishers

Minority Student Involvement in Campus-Based Activities

A primary means by which predominantly white institutions are able to affect the retention rates of students of color is by encouraging them to become more involved in campus activities, become more concerned about student quality-of-life issues, and participate in faculty and administrative decision-making bodies (Pascarella and Terenzini, 1991).

One might assume that when students, or, more specifically, students of color, arrive on campuses, these students are prepared to become involved in all aspects of campus life. But many first-time college or university students enter the institutional setting never having had the experience of participating in student-related school activities. This lack of participation and involvement is considered by many students as an indication of the manner in which their secondary schools have failed to prepare them to take on the positive challenges of college life. However, masses of ethnic minority students throughout the country in secondary schools and institutions are now forcing society to reconsider and reevaluate the education process as they question the current mode of education, try to define their own modes, and attempt to exert some control over their own learning and social environment.

The historic era of student activism on college or university campuses ended around the mid 1970s. This era produced marked changes relative to student involvement and participation in campus governance issues (Schlesinger and Baldridge, 1982). Although these patterns of participation vary from campus to campus, such participation is generally considered commonplace for majority students on college and university campuses.

High participation rates may hold for majority students in our institutions, however the research literature indicates that this type of mainstream participation in campus governance issues and, more important, involvement in student activities does not, in general, characterize the campus experiences of ethnic minority students. For example, Pounds (1987) asserted that student affairs practitioners frequently pose two questions when they are discussing the collegiate experiences of African American students: How do black students' collegiate experiences differ from those of white college students? and What impact do those differences have on student affairs programming? Pounds compared and contrasted the differences between black students' and white students' collegiate experiences, finding, in general, that black students are less satisfied with and involved in campus life. Stikes (1984) also contended that black students are less satisfied with college than are their white counterparts because they do not participate in activities that are directly related to their life experiences.

In order to promote involvement, it is incumbent on administrators, faculty, and especially student personnel staff to provide opportunities for ethnic minority students to assume leadership roles on campus, thereby increasing their involvement and visibility as student leaders. Furthermore, it is extremely important for student development specialists to acquire information pertaining to the level of activity and participation exhibited by minority students in relation to student governance.

In a one-year follow-up study of first-year students, Bowman and Wool-bright (1989) found that participation in various campus programs bears on retention rates of both white and black undergraduate students. Among the specific programs or services related to white students' retention was attendance at a union dance or concert, whereas for black students whether or not they had "considered participation in a union recreation trip" significantly correlated with the likelihood that they were still enrolled at the institution one year later. Unfortunately, there were not enough Asian American students in the sample to study the effect of union programs on their retention rates (Ahuna and Mallinckrodt, 1989).

All groups of students need to feel that they are important constituencies within the institution and that they matter. This recognition requires that students be empowered to become involved within the campus community. Empowerment enables students to feel that they are important, and that their involvement in campus activities not only benefits them but also contributes to the campus environment (Williams, 1987).

Krumbein (1989) stated that student power and participation in school governance can benefit all members of the school community but only if students, especially oppressed groups (for example, blacks, Hispanics, and Asians), are able to make the school policies and programs more directly responsive to them—the clients—rather than to powerful white educators and only if youth, blacks, Hispanics, and others are able to participate meaningfully.

The extent to which students in general and members of oppressed groups in particular are able to participate in shared power determines the degree to which the above considerations can be met. If students control only student activities, if blacks determine only the curricula of black studies programs, then they will realize only limited benefits from their limited power and participation. If, however, students also help determine hiring policies, curricula, and evaluation procedures, their influence will be broader and more significant (Pounds, 1987).

Cultural and Social Impact on Student Participation and Involvement

The call during the 1980s was for increased pluralism within higher education. Pluralism suggests more than merely combining different student subgroups; it also means addressing their special needs and concerns. Further, as these subgroups adapt to the campus community, they should not be forced to give up their histories, traditions, and cultural heritages in the interest of creating a student melting pot, which blurs all of the distinctions among different groups. To support the concept of student pluralism is, in effect, to argue that the institution should seek ways to meet the special needs of student subpopulations while fostering a peaceful coexistence among them (Astin, 1982).

The 1992 American Council on Education status report on minority student participation in higher education indicates that "men of color and women of color registered nearly equal gains during the 1990–91 period. Overall, minority men recorded a 8.8 percent enrollment increase, while the rate for minority women increased by 9.4 percent. African American men, long underrepresented in higher education, accounted for an increase of 6.5 percent, for this period" (Carter and Wilson, 1993, p. 6). According to Thomas (1981), black collegiate enrollment witnessed a dramatic increase during the late 1960s, topping out at 8.4 percent of the total college population in 1971 and increasing steadily until the late 1970s. During this time period, black enrollment began to decline.

Feelings of social isolation can be devastating to black students, affecting them psychologically and academically. In this arena black students face, perhaps most acutely, the conflict between entering the mainstream and preserving their cultural identity (Bowman and Woolbright, 1989). The lack of specific programs, offices, and policies designed to address their needs only enhances their feelings of alienation. College unions and student activities can focus on certain issues to change this situation: How are black students recruited to student organizations? What organizations do black students join? Are black students encouraged to join student government and organizations as well as academic clubs (Bowman and Woolbright, 1989)?

African Americans are not the only students to experience difficulties on campus once they enroll. Hispanic and Asian students also suffer from similar problems as well as other problems unique to their groups. For Hispanics, a continuing trend has been an alarmingly large high school dropout rate, in turn negatively affecting their enrollment rates in postsecondary institutions.

The high school completion rates for whites and African Americans exhibited slight declines in 1991, primarily caused by lower completion rates among men. The gender gap also has widened among Hispanics. In 1990, there were positive signs that this gap was narrowing. However, among both men and women, the decline was somewhat greater for Hispanics and African Americans than for whites. Carter and Wilson (1993, p. 7) noted that the decline in completion rates was most notable among Hispanics, where the rate for men dropped six percentage points to a record low of 47.8 percent in 1991, the lowest completion rate for Hispanic men since the Census Bureau first began collecting data on Hispanics in 1972. The Asian American high school population enjoyed the largest high school completion rate in 1991. Their completion rate was higher than that for whites and for the general U.S. population. The completion rate for American Indians was the lowest among the four major ethnic minority groups. This group completed high school at a rate ten percentage points below the rest of the nation's eighteen- to twenty-four-year-old population (Carter and Wilson, 1993, p. 7).

Higher education experts have a number of theories about why so many Hispanics drop out of school. The factors include a high rate of poverty and the low expectations that some teachers have for Hispanic youngsters. In addition, the parents of many Hispanic teenagers do not finish high school themselves and may have trouble helping their children with schoolwork (Mangan, 1992).

If Hispanic students are to function in competitive Anglo-dominated college environments, they must arrive on campus with highly developed assertiveness skills. In traditional Hispanic culture, assertive behaviors are viewed as rude and dishonorable, especially when directed toward elders. Success in a college or a university requires that students feel comfortable with their ability to participate in intellectual debate and discourse, both with other students and with professors. Precollege training in the arts of assertiveness and debate can help these students develop self-esteem and integrity (Pounds, 1987).

The Hispanic population of the United States is growing rapidly, both from birth rate and from immigration. All Americans need to become more aware of Hispanic culture, which represents a significant facet of our national identity.

Bustamante, Carlson, and Chavez (1989) believe that multicultural programs benefit students who are involved in their planning and implementation, as well as involved in the entire campus community. Through identification with the richness of their own backgrounds, students can strengthen their own ethnic pride. Pride in their individual and cultural identities can increase students' potential for success. The development of cultural pride can enhance self-esteem, an area in which minority students experience difficulties. A strengthening of cultural pride among Hispanic students can also help to eradicate many of the myths and stereotypes that have been so damaging to them.

Campus programming with Hispanic students can be a rewarding experience. The richness of the Hispanic cultures can enhance the learning environment of institutions. Because all multicultural experiences should be accessible to the entire campus community, university personnel must develop such programs with Hispanic students, not for them (Bustamante, Carlson, and Chavez, 1989).

Asian Americans are the fastest growing American minority group in higher education institutions, in part because of the recent influx of immigrants and also because of their success in completing high school. Educators must recognize the importance of finding ways to put aside stereotypes and gain a better understanding of the experiences and concerns of Asian Americans.

To meet the needs of Asian American students and contribute to a heightened awareness of all groups on campus, we must design programs that are sensitive to the cultural differences among Asian groups, provide information that reflects the cultural and historical experiences of Asians, invite students to participate without putting them into uncomfortable "spotlight" positions (asking a Japanese American student, for example, to speak in a representational role for all Japanese students), and involve Asian faculty, staff, and community members in the effort as much as possible (Ahuna and Mallinckrodt, 1989). Asian American students participate in many college and community organizations. Ideally, such contacts provide an opportunity to interact with individuals who share similar values, a sense of validation in the personal struggle for college or university achievement, and models for success in the campus setting. Practitioners working with Asian American students should know about such student resources and how they are utilized as social support systems (Chew and Ogi, 1987).

Some students from South Asia have reported that they feel alone on campus, that they are culturally isolated, and that they have difficulty adjusting to college or university life because of the stereotypical views and expectations others have of them. For example, people often assume that all Asian American students are foreigners and compliment them on how well they speak English. Furthermore, many students, regardless of their specific ethnicity or generation, are automatically expected to excel academically and must cope with the pressure of needing to do well in school. Failure is a personal shame that can also reflect on one's family. Many Asian groups have learned that avoiding attention helps them to survive in this country. In many cases, Asian Americans are still reluctant to stand out, for fear of inviting ridicule or hostility (Ahuna and Mallinckrodt, 1989).

Clearly, Asian Americans desire to reach their full potential in college, independently of campus constraints and cultural biases. Institutions that have the greatest success in educating Asian Americans have recognized specific cultural group needs and responded by developing relevant programs and services. Continued success among all institutions in responding to Asian Americans' academic and social needs can be achieved by involving skilled professionals in high-quality, sensitive programs and services for Asian American students. These programs and services can help Asian Americans expand into all areas of campus life, which benefits the student, the family, and the institution, faculty, and staff (Chew and Ogi, 1987).

Many of the programming interventions aimed at meeting the needs of students of color focus on orientation activities, peer counseling, support groups, minority student organizations, cultural centers and events, and heritage activities. While there are some commonalities among students of color, important differences exist among major racial and ethnic groups. Student affairs professionals need to be aware of these differences and ensure that the specific needs of Asian Americans, African Americans, Hispanics, and the subgroups within each of these groups are met (Bourassa, 1991).

A sense of "belongingness" is important to the retention of minority students on predominantly white campuses. This sense of belonging can be achieved through the creation of a multicultural center, a "place of their own" for minority students to help them feel less isolated from the mainstream. Blacks, Hispanics, and Asians are able to interact with others from the same backgrounds and cultures and to have opportunities to socialize and make friends. The multicultural center can also provide moral support and help in solving students' problems (Stennis-Williams, Terrell, and Haynes, 1988).

A Study of Minority Student Involvement

The primary purpose of our study was to assess the level of involvement and participation of African American, Hispanic American, and Asian American students in student activities and governance in predominantly white institutions. We also obtained information from these populations relating to their levels of noninvolvement on campuses.

Institutional Characteristics. A select group of institutions was of interest in this study: those with representative populations of the student groups whom we wished to survey and with comprehensive student activities programs. Based on these selection criteria, four universities were identified to participate in the study: a four-year private institution, a four-year public research institution, a four-year public institution that is primarily commuter and has no residential facilities, and a four-year public urban institution.

Methodology. Due to the paucity of information pertaining to the assessment of minority student participation in student activities and student governance on college and university campuses, a twenty-nine-question survey instrument was developed to obtain information on the level of student involvement and participation in student governance demonstrated on these campuses.

The questionnaire was administered to 250 undergraduate ethnic minority students who were enrolled at the universities sampled in this study. Student affairs administrators at each institution distributed the questionnaires to every minority student on their campus who elected to participate in this study. All of these students participated on a voluntary basis. While there was no time limit imposed on the completion of the survey, student affairs staff reported that most subjects completed the questionnaire within thirty minutes.

Major Findings. The data were analyzed through a variety of statistical techniques: chi-square tests, analyses of variance, and regression analyses. There were 250 valid surveys. The target population included: 159 (63.6 percent) African Americans, 62 (24.8 percent) Hispanic Americans, 18 (7.2 percent) Asian Americans, and 4 (1.6 percent) American Indians; 7 (2.8 percent) returned questionnaires that did not indicate ethnicity (see Table 5.1). In terms

Table 5.1. Percentage Distribution of Sample Students, by Response to Query on Ethnicity

Ethnicity	N	Percentage of Sample	Percentage of Valid Responses	Cumulative Percentage
African American	159	63.6	65.4	65.4
Hispanic American	62	24.8	25.5	90.9
Asian American	18	7.2	7.4	98.4
American Indian	4	1.6	1.6	100
Unspecified	7	2.8	0.0	

Note: Total sample N = 250.

of academic rank, 13.6 percent of the subjects were first-year students, 20.8 percent were sophomores, 29.6 percent were juniors, and 33.2 percent were seniors; 2.8 percent did not specify their classification. Also, 37.6 percent were males and 61.6 percent were females; .8 percent of the respondents did not specify gender.

The subjects were asked to respond to several questions pertaining to their involvement and membership affiliation with student organizations (see Table 5.2), the length of time of active membership, and the level of time committed to working with campus student organizations primarily on a weekly basis. Based on a chi-square test, significant patterns emerged from the 131 African American students who responded to the question "How involved are you in campus student organizations?" We found that 51 (39 percent) were not involved, 48 (37 percent) were somewhat involved, and 32 (24 percent) were very involved. Among the 57 Hispanic students who responded to this question, 12 (21 percent) were not involved, 26 (46 percent) were somewhat involved, and 19 (33 percent) were very involved. Of the 14 Asian American students who responded, 5 (36 percent) were not involved, 3 (21 percent) were somewhat involved, and 6 (43 percent) were very involved.

These findings suggest that when ethnicity is viewed in terms of involvement in campus organizations, African American and Hispanic American students are somewhat involved in student organizations, but not at the same level as Asian American students. Even though the sample size of Asian students in this study was small, national retention reports show that Asian students tend to accomplish more by group participation, thereby demonstrating a higher level of involvement in their own ethnic student organizations.

In regard to subjects' responses to queries about their involvement in student governance and participation in ethnic student organizations, 79 subjects indicated that they did not actively participate in student governance and were not active members of campus organizations. There were significant differences in the responses of subjects related to their perceptions of what the primary role of student organizations should be on campuses: 119 (48 percent) thought that promoting cultural diversity was important, 44 (18 percent) felt that estab-

Table 5.2. Percentage Distribution of Sample Students, by Response to Query on Organizational Affiliation

Type of Organization	N	Percentage of Sample	Percentage of Valid Responses	Cumulative Percentage
Political	60	24.0	35.1	35.1
Academic	31	12.4	18.1	53.2
Greek	21	8.4	12.3	65.5
Athletic	3	1.2	1.8	67.3
Club	56	22.4	32.7	100
No affiliation	79	31.6	0	

Note: Total sample N = 250.

lishing communication with the administration was paramount, 16 (6 percent) stated that promoting leadership was at the forefront of the organizations' agendas, and 13 (5 percent) indicated that making the organizations visible on campus was extremely important.

A chi-square test indicated significant differences in relation to ethnicity of subjects and perceptions of faculty and staff sensitivity to minority student issues on campus. The general perceptions of the subjects were as follows: (1) Out of 95 African American students who responded, 38 (40 percent) felt that the faculty and staff were insensitive to minority issues, 41 (43 percent) felt that faculty and staff were somewhat sensitive to minority issues, and 16 (17 percent) felt that the faculty and staff were sensitive to minority issues. (2) Of the 36 Hispanic American students who responded, 11 (31 percent) felt that the faculty and staff were insensitive to minority issues, 12 (33 percent) felt that the faculty and staff were somewhat sensitive to minority issues, and 13 (36 percent) felt that the faculty and staff were sensitive to minority issues. (3) Out of 13 Asian American students who responded, 3 (23 percent) felt that the faculty and staff were insensitive to minority issues, 4 (31 percent) felt that faculty and staff were somewhat sensitive to minority issues, and 6 (46 percent) felt that the faculty and staff were sensitive to minority issues. (4) All 4 (100 percent) Indian Americans felt that the faculty and staff were insensitive to minority issues.

The results from this analysis suggest that views on the importance of minority student involvement and participation and on the critical issues that minority students confront vary from person to person. In general, as perceived by the students, faculty's and staff's attitudes toward minority student governance issues and their involvement to resolve these issues were somewhat important, but it is obvious from these data that minority student issues were not at the top of their priority lists.

The subjects also responded to several questions related to their participation in student leadership training and activities. Out of the 250 subjects surveyed, a total of 105 (42 percent) indicated that they had been involved and had participated in leadership development and training activities. In contrast, 138 subjects (55 percent) stated that they had not participated in any leadership training activities. Seven of the subjects did not respond to this question. There was no significant relationship found between ethnicity (race) and participation in leadership training. Most subjects who responded to these questions felt that the development of leadership skills was important.

Subjects also were asked about the level of emphasis that should be placed on the development of various leadership skills (for example, communication skills, thinking independently, problem solving, organizing work projects, delegating authority, budgeting, and developing personal values) while participating in college student organizations. A total of 247 subjects responded to this question: 193 (78 percent) of the subjects felt that great emphasis should be placed on the development of these skills, 48 (19 percent) indicated moderate emphasis, 5 (2 percent) slight, and 1 (.4 percent) indicated that no emphasis should be placed on this type of leadership development.

Discussion

The results from this study support previous research indicating that a lack of involvement by minority students in campus activities can produce negative retention rates (Astin, 1982; Pounds, 1987; Tinto, 1975). Fleming (1984) also found that covert and overt racism in faculty-student relations creates a climate of hostility and rejection for African Americans and other minorities.

As indicated by the data of this study, the perceptions of the subjects regarding the feelings of faculty, staff, and their peers in relation to minority student governance issues were borderline. Overall, the subjects felt that faculty and staff were somewhat sensitive to minority student issues pertaining to student government. However, there were also negative attitudes and comments conveyed as to the insensitivity displayed by faculty and staff in relation to minority student governance issues. The different ethnic groups, however, had different perceptions regarding the feelings of the faculty and staff relative to global minority student issues. These results support the research findings of Fleming (1984) and others.

Additional findings of this study are that the kind of student organizations in which the students were involved depended on their ethnic backgrounds, and that there was not much student participation in student organizations, especially not across ethnic lines, that is, there was not much cross-cultural interaction occurring across groups of minority students and their organizations on some campuses. These data suggest the need for mechanisms to break down existing barriers that impede the progress of communication and assimilation.

A variety of approaches can help promote cross-cultural involvement and interaction: (1) Conduct regular joint meetings with all ethnic minority student organization leaders. This intervention should focus on group dynamics, interaction, and the development of communication skills. (2) Support at least two or three social activities per year that require all ethnic minority student organizations to participate. These events are appealing to many students and are excellent means for promoting diversity and cross-cultural understanding. (3) Provide opportunities for ethnic minority student organizations to conduct forums that address contemporary social issues and the organizations' particular concerns. Forums of this kind provide excellent arenas for exchange and dialogue. The forums should be marketed and widely advertised among all of the student population. (4) Develop programs for ethnic minority students to showcase their organizations' missions and purposes. Even a one-day program can provide an opportunity for more students to become aware of what an organization has to offer. Although many of these approaches and recommendations are already in place on many campuses, a continual emphasis on promoting interaction and dialogue can enhance the likelihood that students will become involved, or more involved, in student governance activities.

As Williams (1987) suggested, student affairs practitioners can no longer prevent minority student homogeneity on college campuses. There must be mechanisms created on campuses to promote cross-cultural interaction and awareness. The studies cited in this chapter point out the importance of learning about different groups' customs, values, and linguistic styles, since this serves to enhance one's understanding of individuals from ethnic backgrounds different from one's own. A primary means of accomplishing this mutual understanding is the promotion of minority student involvement in student organizations, student governance, and campus programming activities. Much of the research literature suggests that when students—in particular, ethnic minority students—are involved on a predominantly white campus, they feel a sense of belonging and believe that they are a part of the culture on that campus (Pounds, 1987).

Another essential aspect of the present study concerned leadership and the level at which ethnic minority students are involved in developing skills to become leaders or exercising skills that are already developed. Lavant, Brown, and Newsome (1992, p. 165) contended that "students who hold leadership positions play a very important role in their institution's future. Much of their leadership influences the type of campus environment and nature of the student body."

Our respondents' answers to the question about student leadership training and activities revealed that this group of ethnic minority students was cognizant of the importance of participating in leadership development activities. Moreover, it was also evident from their responses that the development of leadership skills was of significant importance to them. Perhaps these students were attempting to develop skills with the hope that they would be able to apply them in a leadership role within a campus organization.

Conclusion

The implications of our findings are broad. It is apparent from the responses of the subjects who participated in our study that they were involved and participating in student governance activities in a limited manner. In order for an institution to reach its goals and for ethnic minority students to achieve their full potential, student affairs professionals, faculty, and staff must continue to encourage this population to be active participants in the day-to-day activities that affect their lives as students. They must be encouraged to assume leadership roles and take advantage of leadership opportunities. They must continually be made aware that this type of involvement and participation will enhance their chances of having a successful college or university experience.

Past research on the effects of ethnic minority students' interaction with other groups on predominantly white campuses indicates that African American, Hispanic American, and Asian American students who take on leadership roles on campus and in student organizations enhance their relationships with one another and their white peers. This finding defines not only a vision for student affairs personnel but also a goal for all involved in higher education and the education of ethnic minority students.

References

Ahuna, L., and Mallinckrodt, B. "Asian Americans." In C. Woolbright (ed.), *Valuing Diversity on Campus: A Multicultural Approach.* Bloomington, Ind.: Association of College Unions-International, 1989.

Astin, A. W. *Minorities in American Higher Education: Recent Trends, Current Prospects, and Recommendations.* San Francisco: Jossey-Bass, 1982.

Bourassa, D. M. "How White Students and Students of Color Organize and Interact on Campus." In J. C. Dalton (ed.), *Racism on Campus: Confronting Racial Bias Through Peer Interventions.* New Directions for Student Services, no. 56. San Francisco: Jossey-Bass, 1991.

Bowman, R., and Woolbright, C. "Black Americans." In C. Woolbright (ed.), *Valuing Diversity on Campus: A Multicultural Approach.* Bloomington, Ind.: Association of College Unions-International, 1989.

Bustamante, M., Carlson, J., and Chavez, E. "Hispanic Americans." In C. Woolbright (ed.), *Valuing Diversity on Campus: A Multicultural Approach.* Bloomington, Ind.: Association of College Unions-International, 1989.

Carter, D. J., and Wilson, R. "Minorities in Higher Education." In *Eleventh Annual Status Report.* Washington, D.C.: American Council on Education, 1993.

Chew, C. A., and Ogi, A. Y. "Asian American College Student Perspectives." In D. J. Wright (ed.), *Responding to the Needs of Today's Minority Students.* New Directions for Student Services, no. 38. San Francisco: Jossey-Bass, 1987.

Fleming, J. "Special Needs of Blacks and Other Minorities." In A. W. Chickering and Associates, *The Modern American College: Responding to the New Realities of Diverse Students and a Changing Society.* San Francisco: Jossey-Bass, 1981.

Fleming, J. *Blacks in College: A Comparative Study of Students' Success in Black and in White Institutions.* San Francisco: Jossey-Bass, 1984.

Hughes, M. "Black Students' Participation in Higher Education." *Journal of College Student Personnel,* 1987, *28,* 532.

Jones, W. T. "Enhancing Minority-White Peer Interactions." In D. J. Wright (ed.), *Responding to the Needs of Today's Minority Students.* New Directions for Student Services, no. 38. San Francisco: Jossey-Bass, 1987.

Krumbein, G. "Student Leadership Groups at the Middle Level: Turning a School Around." *NASSP Bulletin,* 1989, pp. 40–45.

Lavant, B. D., Brown, C. L., and Newsome, E. "Perceptions and Views of Racism: A Student Leader's Perspective." In M. C. Terrell (ed.), *Diversity, Disunity, and Campus Community.* Washington, D.C.: National Association of Student Personnel Administrators, 1992.

Mangan, K. S. "Despite Enrollment Gains, Hispanics' College Going Rate Changes Little in Decade." *Chronicle of Higher Education,* Feb. 26, 1992, pp. A36–A37.

Pascarella, E. T., and Terenzini, P. T. *How College Affects Students: Findings and Insights from Twenty Years of Research.* San Francisco: Jossey-Bass, 1991.

Pounds, A. W. "Black Students' Needs on Predominantly White Campuses." In D. J. Wright (ed.), *Responding to the Needs of Today's Minority Students.* New Directions for Student Services, no. 38. San Francisco: Jossey-Bass, 1987.

Schlesinger, S., and Baldridge, J. V. "Is Student Power Dead in Higher Education?" *College Student Journal,* 1982, *16,* 9–17.

Stennis-Williams, S. S., Terrell, M. C., and Haynes, A. "The Emergent Role of Multicultural Education Centers on Predominantly White Campuses." In M. C. Terrell and D. J. Wright (eds.), *From Survival to Success: Promoting Minority Student Retention.* Washington, D.C.: National Association of Student Personnel Administrators, 1988.

Stikes, C. S. *Black Students in Higher Education.* Carbondale: Southern Illinois University Press, 1984.

Thomas, G. E. (ed.). *Black Students in Higher Education: Conditions and Experiences in the 1970s.* Westpoint, Conn.: Greenwood Press, 1981.

Tinto, V. "Dropout from Higher Education: A Theoretical Synthesis of Recent Research." *Review of Educational Research,* 1975, *45* (1), 89–125.

Williams, D. J. "Minority Students: Developmental Beginnings." In D. J. Wright (ed.), *Responding to the Needs of Today's Minority Students.* New Directions for Student Services, no. 38. San Francisco: Jossey-Bass, 1987.

BRUCE D. LAVANT is director of the preparatory division and adjunct assistant professor of educational and counseling psychology at the University of Louisville, Louisville, Kentucky.

MELVIN C. TERRELL is vice president for student affairs and professor of counselor education at Northeastern Illinois University, Chicago. He was a 1993–1994 American Council on Education Fellow at Florida State University.

In the study reported here, student governments members and their constituents were asked to indicate what services were being provided on their campuses, the effectiveness of these programs, and which issues they considered most important.

Student Government as a Provider of Student Services

Michael J. Cuyjet

Although sometimes viewed as peripheral in the structure of the campus governance, student governments on many campuses are the essential, and often the sole, providers of certain services on which students have come to rely. As Barr, Keating, and Associates (1985, p. 5) stated, "All student services programs—whether major administrative units, a series of activities, or a one-time event—attempt to fulfill one or more of three overarching purposes: to provide essential institutional services, to teach life management skills, and to provide links through which students can integrate knowledge gained in both the curricular and co-curricular settings." To achieve these purposes, all of the members of the campus administrative community—student affairs personnel, student leaders, academic leaders, faculty, and staff—endeavor to make a substantive contribution, for such a pooling of resources is needed to provide the full range of programs and activities that an institution might wish to offer. In such an environment, student government becomes a fully participating partner in the effort to provide a supportive milieu for the student body.

This chapter examines student government's role as the vehicle through which students' issues are addressed and their cocurricular needs are met. The chapter begins with a brief review of the different structures of student governments and the role of student government as a service provider throughout the history of higher education in the United States. Then, the results of a study are presented, revealing students' perceptions about their student governments' roles in providing services. Topics on the survey included the issues that students felt were being addressed, the relative effectiveness of services provided, and students' ideas about which issues were truly important to their campus communities. The implications of these responses are also discussed.

NEW DIRECTIONS FOR STUDENT SERVICES, no. 66, Summer 1994 © Jossey-Bass Publishers

Typically, student government's major function is to serve as the "official" voice of the student body to the institution's administrators. As such, student government leaders conduct their own elections and appoint representatives to the various committees and deliberative bodies within the school's administrative structure. Student government also, typically, plays a central role in the allocation of student activities fees to other organizations and agencies. However, besides representing the student body to the administration and allocating student activities fees, student governments across the country provide a wide variety of other services. These services often include the administrative duties of officially recognizing other student organizations and programming extracurricular activities. Some student governments provide "social" services such as printing and circulating teacher evaluations, organizing voter registration drives, and addressing societal needs such as homelessness, hunger, and inadequate child care. Even programs such as legal aid offices, book exchanges, and travel agencies are established and run by student governments for their constituencies. Student governments also get involved in issues that require an advocacy role beyond the campus governance structure. Student government officers occasionally address student-related issues with municipal, county, or state governments and participate at a variety of levels, from attending meetings, to circulating petitions, to organizing and conducting rallies. Student governments may even get involved in the external political activities affecting the institutions (Chiles and Pruitt, 1985).

Student Government Structure

In order to explore the roles that student governments play in providing services to their campus communities, it is important, first, to examine the ways in which student governments are structured and how they relate to the administrative organizations on their respective campuses. Although there are numerous forms of student government, there appear to be three general models that define the method of interaction with the institution's governance structure. The most prevalent model is an independent student government, consisting of students alone and concerned chiefly with administering student activities and often called upon to present the "student perspective" to the institution's administration. A second model is community governance, in which students join faculty and staff in an administrative body, sharing the responsibilities and powers of running the institution. Within this model there exists a range of roles for student members, from fully functioning participants with voting power and executive responsibilities to largely ceremonial posts without vote or real voice. The third model is a combination of the first two, in which students participate in the governance of the institution with a separate government of their own as well as with a voice in the school's community governing body. Usually, some formal link exists between these two entities, such as a structure in which the student membership of the community government is selected by the officers of the independent government, who in turn are elected by the student body at large.

Klopf (1960) further defined the first model in identifying four categories of self-government: the student council, the organizational council, the bicameral government, and the student association. The student council (or student government association or other, similar name) is a representative body in which the members are selected by the student body as a whole or each member is chosen by a certain segment of the student body, such as a residence unit. The organizational council consists of representatives of various recognized campus organizations or groups. It is usually composed of the heads of these campus organizations and is chiefly responsible for administering policies that affect the operation of these groups, particularly funding for their programs. The bicameral student government consists of two entities, one a relatively small group having executive and some legislative powers and the other a larger assembly concerned solely with legislation. Some student governments employing this form of government add a third component, emulating our federal government with a judicial agency to become tricameral. The student association is an organization in which there is a clear, direct relationship between the government agency and the student body. Such a structure may have a small governing group, but it is perceived as merely a legislative council for the group as a whole. In some student associations every enrolled student is considered a member, while in others students must initiate some action, such as paying a fee, to be members. Obviously, among the hundreds of schools, there are forms of student government that combine the features of these general categories. What is important, however, is that the student government afford its members the opportunity to provide services and programs for the campus to employ as part of the cocurriculum.

Student Government's History as a Service Provider

The functions and services provided by student government have fluctuated over centuries and continue to evolve as the influence of students on the collegiate environment ebbs and flows and as the needs of the constituents change. Since a history of student government is presented in Golden and Schwartz (this volume), a comprehensive review is unnecessary here. However, it is appropriate to highlight a few of the interesting examples of various services offered by student government since medieval times. The role of student government has swung like a pendulum from complete autonomy in the operation of various components of the education institution to virtual inactivity in the face of an autocratic administration. Actually, some of the earliest known examples of student self-governance are also among the most comprehensive.

> The first medieval universities were owned and operated by the students, who hired the faculty, chose the towns in which the universities were set up, formulated the rules by which the schools were governed, and dealt directly with the municipalities when difficulties arose. . . . Foreign students in a strange city had neither civil nor political rights, and their own governments made little or no provision for their protection. Groups based on national affiliation therefore

> banded together as "nations." Each of these "nations" was chartered by the university's sponsor. The students, so organized, controlled the universities. The "nations" constituted the real governing authority of the university, for they made decisions upon policies, housing, routines, fees, and schedules, and took charge of all cases of discipline, whether the infraction of the rule was "gown" or "town" [Falvey, 1952, p. 34].

The thirteenth-century University of Bologna was thought to be possibly the best example of this model (Lunn, 1957). The entire university was administered by the assemblies of nations. Even the university rector had to be a student and could not be more than twenty-five years old (Falvey, 1952).

This democratic ideal was certainly not present in early American higher education. From the mid eighteenth century to the mid nineteenth century, the most common forms of organized student activities were literary clubs and debating societies. The literary societies developed such strong loyalty among their members that they began to serve a judicial role in disciplining students whose behaviors violated organizational, dormitory, or community rules or brought disgrace to fellow society members. In these efforts to control themselves, the groups represented a rudimentary type of student government (Saddlemire, 1988). In a 1899 study of twenty small New England colleges and twenty of the largest universities, five distinct areas of student participation were found: student courts for those caught cheating on examinations, advisory committees to the faculty, committees with general disciplinary powers, committees for the maintenance of dormitories, and student organizations to "unify and make representative all student interests" (Falvey, 1952, p. 42).

Changes in higher education following World War I allowed many student groups, including student governments, to flourish during this time (Saddlemire, 1988), but their functions were still limited mainly to supervising student social activities, maintaining the honor system, and handling disciplinary cases (Falvey, 1952). The upsurge of activism occurring in the late 1960s and early 1970s was a major factor creating a significant change in the nature of student government and its influence on campus governance in the twentieth century. Student government leaders came to assume greater responsibility in providing constituent services. Several catalysts, including the large numbers of "baby boom" children arriving at their college-age years, the motivation provided by the civil rights movement, and the unpopularity of the Vietnam War and the students' reactions to it, all contributed to a movement that demanded greater control by students over their own activities, affairs, and policies (see Lavant and Terrell, this volume, for detailed exploration of this subject).

To summarize, the three main purposes of student government that have developed over the history of higher education are to assume certain responsibilities that the institution's administration is willing to share (either voluntarily or reluctantly), to provide leadership experiences for those involved in the government process that are directly beneficial to those students, and to provide valuable cocurricular services for the student body. This chapter explores the third purpose of student government listed here by examining those services provided by student leaders for their constituent student bodies.

A Study of Student Governments as Service Providers

To examine the role of student governments as service providers, an empirical study was conducted to solicit information about basic services from students at several hundred colleges and universities across the country.

Methodology. To gather data regarding the different issues addressed by student governments at institutions across the country and the programs and services provided by these student governments, a quantitative survey instrument was developed, listing a sample of issues that student governments are known to address at American colleges and universities. More than one hundred different issues were considered, but to make the survey a more reasonable length for respondents, the final list consisted of fifty-one items determined to be representative of the important issues on a majority of campuses across the country (see Appendix of this chapter). The list was formulated by examination of similar instruments used in previous research (Cuyjet, 1985; Keppler and Robinson, 1993) and by review of a panel of administrators and student leaders.

The target sample was determined to be two students each at approximately three hundred schools. Rather than mail the surveys directly to student government leaders, I assumed that a greater rate of return would be realized if the instruments were sent to each institution's chief student affairs officer (CSAO) with a request that he or she personally ask two student leaders to complete the forms. Each CSAO who received the mailing was asked to give one questionnaire to a student active in student government and one student who was not, or had never been, involved in student government, in order to provide a less subjective element to the assessment.

Surveys of this type present a dilemma regarding the objectivity of the responses. Asking student government officers about the issues they face and the services they provide is necessary, since they are the best sources of information about what programs are being administered by student government on campus. However, their proximity to the issues and their decision-making authority with respect to which programs are offered can yield a skewed perspective of the relative importance of these issues to the student body as a whole. To test this concern about the objectivity of self-reports on the effectiveness of student government's attention to the issues by those students who are involved directly in student government, an important component of this survey was the posing of the same questions regarding the services provided and their effectiveness to a sample of students *not* involved at all with the student government organizations.

Respondents were asked to indicate whether or not they held at that time, or had previously held, an elected or appointed position in their respective school's student government. Each was then requested to indicate which of the listed issues had been addressed by his or her student government over the prior year. Since this survey was conducted in the fall semester, current student leaders may not have had ample time to establish new programs in the current academic year. This second request was thus also an attempt to focus on those issues that evoked continuity in programming rather than those that might be only the "pet projects" of a current student government administration. Respondents were also asked to indicate how effective their student governments had been in addressing each issue identified from the list. Finally, each respondent was asked to rank the three most important of these issues and services.

Results were analyzed with simple frequency counts, using the entire sample and after dividing it according to the response regarding involvement in student government. Statistical significance of the comparisons of responses between the two groups was at the $p < .05$ level. A series of chi-square analyses was employed to test for significance. Overall, 389 completed surveys were returned by the time the data analysis began. Of these, 215 respondents indicated that they were holding, or had held, student government positions, while 171 indicated that they had never held such a position; 3 respondents failed to provide this information.

Results: Most Prevalent Services and Issues. The first examination of the data was a review of which items among the entire sample yielded the greatest number of responses (yes or no) to the question "Your student government has been involved with the issue over the past year." Each of the ten most popular responses received a positive response from more than three-fourths of the sample. Table 6.1 lists those items.

The ten items that received the least affirmations by all respondents (low-

Table 6.1. Rankings of Most Prevalent Student Government Services and Issues as Indicated by Respondents in Government and Not in Government

Issue/Item	All Respondents		In Government		Not in Government	
Representation on campuswide committees	1	(89.6)	1	(94.4)	2	(83.1)
Acitvities programming	2	(86.8)	4	(88.7)	1	(84.2)
Allocation of student activity fees	3	(84.5)	2	(90.2)	6	(76.7)
Recognition or registration of student organizations	4	(84.0)	5	(87.8)	4	(79.4)
Participation in college or university governance	5	(83.9)	7	(86.8)	3	(79.9)
Multicultural awareness and diversity	6	(81.7)	6	(86.9)	7	(74.7)
Representation on the college or university council or senate	7	(81.0)	8	(85.8)	8	(74.2)
Safety on campus	8	(80.3)	10	(82.2)	5	(77.6)
Recycling and environmental issues	9	(78.6)	9	(84.2)	9	(71.1)
General student apathy	10	(77.4)	3	(88.8)	14	(62.0)

Note: Parenthetical figures are the percentages of respondents answering yes to the question "Your student government has been involved with the issue over the past year."

est to highest) were administrative and faculty salaries (13.8 percent), organizing national lobbies (17 percent), drug use and testing (17.1 percent), enrollment ceilings (17.7 percent), faculty and staff collective bargaining (17.8 percent), admissions standards (25.6 percent), legal aid (26 percent), day care for students (26.7 percent), graduation standards (27.9 percent), and community homelessness (29.4 percent). The merit of this list is not that a relatively small percentage of student governments were reported to be addressing these issues but that *some students* were involving themselves in these issues, up to more than one-quarter of the respondents on this survey. These are matters not easily addressed or, for some student governments, not within their typical purview. However, it is encouraging that some student governments are participating in the attention their campuses are giving to these less salient matters, which were still of consequence to the student body, directly or indirectly.

Responses of Student Government Participants. Survey respondents indicated whether or not they were currently, or had previously been, holders of elected or appointed positions in student government. This variable was a test of the hypothesis that students not directly involved in student government had a statistically significant different perception of the services provided and the issues addressed by student government and the effectiveness with which those services and issues were handled.

The review of the responses from the in-government group to the first question, whether or not the fifty-one items listed were or were not addressed on the respondent's campus, yielded results very similar to those for the entire sample. In fact, the top ten popular items were the same, only the order was changed slightly (see Table 6.1). Representation on campuswide committees was, again, the item receiving the greatest percentage of yes responses (94.4 percent); allocation of student activity fees, which had been third among all respondents, was second (90.2 percent) among in-government students. All the other items, save one, moved only one or two places in the ranking. Even the percentages of positive responses were only 1.9 to 5.8 points different from those generated by the entire sample. The one item that made a significant shift was general student apathy. It had been the tenth-ranked item among all respondents (77.4 percent), but it had the third highest percentage of affirmative responses (88.8 percent) among those students involved in student government.

This issue of apathy was the most volatile among the list presented on the survey. As discussed above, this issue had a relatively low effectiveness rating compared to its ranking as a popular item. As discussed below, the not-in-government students ranked it much lower. In fact, the rating given to this issue by the students involved in student government is the anomaly within the survey. Almost nine out of ten student government leaders in this survey identified student apathy as an issue that they addressed. Yet their not-in-government constituents did not agree that it was addressed nearly that much, and only around six out of ten in either group felt that it was being addressed effectively. Either the student government members were worrying far too much about this concern, compared to its impact on the student body, or a considerably large minority of the students surveyed felt that since not much could be done about apathy, there were other issues deserving greater attention, especially some that were being addressed more effectively.

On the other end of the continuum, the list of least-mentioned items also stayed relatively the same for the in-government group as for the sample as a whole. The issue of off-campus housing was slightly ahead of community homelessness as the tenth of ten items receiving the lowest percentages of affirmative marks in the survey. A similar pattern developed for the least-mentioned items in the not-in-government group. Nine of the ten items from the entire group were the same, with organizing state or regional lobbies being slightly less popular than graduation standards. This could be seen as a ray of optimism that this group had taken more of an interest in graduate standards, but the margin was not substantial enough to warrant such a conclusion.

Responses of Students Not in Government. As with the in-government group, the top ten responses to the question of which items were being addressed from the students not in government largely reflected the responses from the entire sample. Again, nine of the first ten responses were the same, although each may have shifted as many as four places in the ranking (see Table 6.1). Among the not-in-government students, activities programming (84.1 percent) was ranked first (it was second among all respondents, and fourth among those in government), representation on campuswide committees (83.1 percent) was second (it was first in the other two rankings), and participation in college or university governance (79.9 percent) was third (as compared to rankings of eighth and seventh, respectively, in the other lists). Safety on campus was given a higher ranking as the fifth most popular issue, possibly indicating that the students not in government saw attention being paid to this matter and gave more credit to student government for this concern than the positional leaders claimed. Finally, as mentioned above, general student apathy was identified as an issue being addressed by a much lower percentage (62 percent) of not-in-government students than their counterparts in government. The issues of sexual assault and date rape, voter registration, alcohol policy and alcohol abuse, and race relations on campus were presented as more popular issues in this survey than was apathy, the fourteenth-ranked item. If student government members were addressing apathy, many of their constituents were not getting the message.

One final observation regarding the frequency of these issues as indicated by the survey responses merits mention. The percentages of not-in-government respondents indicating the presence of these issues on their campuses were consistently a few percentage points lower than the similar responses from the in-government group. The difference was statistically significant ($p <$ .05) for twenty-one of the fifty-one yes-no items. This phenomenon seems to indicate that students who are involved directly in government positions tend to be more aware of the programs and services occurring on campus than are their constituents. This is not new information for anyone, student or staff, who has worked in the student activities area. Publicizing the events and activities of student government as well as the other student agencies providing programming to the student body has been, and continues to be, one of the biggest problems faced by student programmers.

Results: Effectiveness of Services. In addition to marking whether each item was, indeed, an issue being addressed on the campus, each respondent was asked to expand on those items for which he or she answered in the affirmative. If a yes answer was given, the subject was then requested to indicate to what extent the issue was being addressed *effectively*. Subjects were given a range of four choices: greatly effective, somewhat effective, minimally effective, and not effective. To simplify the responses for this analysis, the answers were grouped into two poles: those answering greatly or somewhat effective and those answering minimally or not effective.

All Respondents. A list of the ten items receiving the highest percentages of responses indicating that they were addressed greatly or somewhat effectively contains most of the same items as the list of top yes-or-no items. The order shifted somewhat, and two of the items were not perceived as all that effective. The first four items on the yes-no list (representation on campuswide committees, activities programming, allocation of student activity fees, and recognition or registration of student organizations) were also at the top of the list of those items managed effectively; however, their order changed. Students felt that the most effective service provided by student government was the recognition or registration of student organizations (88.1 percent), followed by activities programming (86.3 percent). Since these are the two items in the top-ten popular list that can be seen to have the most direct effect on the lives of large numbers of students, this result is not surprising. The most popular response, student government's representation on campuswide committees, was seen as only the third most effective service (85.9 percent), ranking slightly ahead of allocation of student fees (85.3 percent). While these functions are, indeed, critical to the operation of the typical student government, their impact is more "in-house" than is apparent to the general student body.

Students felt that safety on campus was the next most effectively addressed service (83.3 percent). Multicultural awareness and diversity, while the sixth most popular issue, was only the ninth-ranked in effectiveness (76.4 percent). This seems to indicate that while the student governments in four out of five schools in this survey were attempting to address the issue of multiculturalism and diversity, one in four of the students at those schools believed that the matter was not being handled effectively. Two other issues from the top-ten popular list that were not perceived as being addressed effectively are recycling and environmental issues and general student apathy. Recycling was deemed effectively addressed by only 68.6 percent of those students who said that it was being faced on their campuses. Apathy was judged as effectively handled by only 64.3 percent of the students who said that it was being addressed. That is a lower effectiveness rating on this survey than given to graduation standards, which was one of the ten least-popular issues on the list. Of course, apathy, while an issue of considerable concern to most student government participants, is not actually a service to the community. Moreover, the judgment of how well it is being addressed is a Catch 22. The greater an issue apathy becomes and the more it is addressed as a problem by student government, the more ineffective student government appears in resolving the issue.

Two other issues that did not rank very high on the popular list were perceived as being addressed effectively, nonetheless. Voter registration was perceived to be addressed effectively by 79.9 percent of the respondents, and sexual assault and date rape was seen as effectively dealt with by 76 percent. This was despite the fact that neither of these items was seen as an issue being addressed on more than two-thirds of the campuses in the survey. Even though a large minority of student governments represented in this study were not reported to be addressing the issue of sexual assault and date rape, it was encouraging that those who were dealing with it were reported by more than three out of four students to be doing an effective job at it.

Respondents Split by Groups. Among both the subgroups of respondents, there was a high correlation for most items between the popularity percentage and the effectiveness percentage. In other words, those items that received a high percentage of yes scores also received a high percentage of scores indicating that the issues were being addressed greatly or somewhat effectively. Yet, there are several exceptions worth noting. While more than 80 percent of student government members rated recycling as an issue being addressed, only 65 percent of them felt that it was being addressed effectively. And while 75 percent of those students saw parking as an issue being addressed, only 59.3 percent saw it as effectively addressed. Several other items, while present on far fewer campuses, were nonetheless judged as being addressed effectively. Voter registration, although marked present by less than two-thirds of the respondents, was deemed effective by 84.9 percent of those students. Only 58.3 percent of the students indicated that they were represented by student government on administrative search committees, but 80 percent of those students found that representation effective. Legal aid services were marked as available by only 28.2 percent of the in-government students, but 63.6 percent found the services effective. Among the students not in government, only a little more than one-half indicated that office space was provided for student organizations, but 81.4 percent found the service effective.

Significant Differences Between Groups. Although this chapter endeavors to illuminate which services were prevalent on a representative sample of college and university campuses, the fact is that these items, with the few exceptions noted, were also the services that were perceived to be effectively delivered. Student government leaders and their advisers observing these data might conclude that effectiveness is a more important criterion by which to judge their programs than is popularity. Indeed, the measure of success of constituent service delivery on a campus ought to be how well these programs are received by the general student body. This message is particularly salient for the eleven items for which the differences in ratings of effectiveness between responses from the in-government and the not-in-government students were statistically significant: allocation of student activity fees, rising tuition, office space for student organizations, representation on the college or university council or senate, representation on campuswide committees, representation on faculty search committees, recognition or registration of student organizations, participation in college or university governance, legal aid, voter registration, and activities programming.

In two cases, rising tuition and office space for student organizations, the not-in-government students expressed a higher effectiveness score than did the in-government group. However, for the other nine items, the students involved in student government felt that they were addressing the matters more effectively than was perceived by their constituents. In isolation, such miscommunication is a minor nuisance. However, if all of these survey scores were to emanate from one hypothetical school, it would be clear that the student government on that campus was critically out of touch. The message for student government members and the staff who advise them is to develop assessments and other means to stay in touch with their constituents and periodically to feel the pulse of the student body in relation to the issues being addressed.

For the first seven items on the list, there were also statistically significant differences between the responses of the in-government group and the not-in-government group to the question of whether the issues were even being addressed on campus. In each case, significantly more students involved in student government indicated that they were addressing the issue than was indicated by their not-in-government counterparts. It is interesting that the four items yielding significant differences in the perceived effectiveness but not in the frequency of addressing the issues, three are what could be termed *direct* services: legal aid, voter registration, and activities programming. Perhaps the direct application of such services helps to make nongovernment constituents more aware of their existence than of the more administrative functions such as representation on committees. Or perhaps the need to directly serve constituents gives student government leaders a more realistic understanding of whether or not they are truly addressing the issues in addition to giving them a measure of their effectiveness in doing so.

Results: Issues Deemed Important. Ultimately, campus student government leaders must make some decision as to what issues are important to the student body. No group can be all things to the entire campus and address all issues. How those decisions are made as to the selection of programs and services is often as important as the actions that follow. To do a tremendous job in producing a program that few people find important or relevant is of little benefit. In addressing this matter of issue salience in the study, I discovered that students' perceptions of what issues are important appeared to be greatly affected by whether or not they were involved directly in student government.

At the conclusion of the survey, each respondent was asked, "Of the issues listed above, which three do you consider to be the most important for student government to address on your campus?" Since the question did not ask students to rank-order their responses, the totals of the top-three responses were added together for purposes of comparison. The results were compiled separately for the two subsets of the study's student sample, based on the subjects' responses to the question regarding holding an elected or appointed position in student government. Although there were a number of issues sharing approximately the same places in the two rankings, this analysis demonstrated that students involved in government and their constituents who were not directly active had markedly different priorities as to what concerns student government ought to be addressing. Among the thirteen items listed in Table 6.2 are the ten items that received the most responses from those students not involved in student government, as well as those items that were among the top ten responses given by students in government.

For student government leaders and their staff and faculty advisers, these are some of the most noteworthy results of this study; there was considerable disagreement as to the relative importance of a number of important issues and services in which student governments are typically involved. The disparity is demonstrated in the first item listed in Table 6.2. By a large margin, students not in government positions indicated that rising tuition was the issue they felt was the most important to be addressed. Yet, this item ranked only eighth among students involved in government. Similarly, the third most important issue for not-in-government respondents, safety on campus, was only the ninth most important issue for government members. Perhaps the student government leaders believed that by attending to the procedural issues of participation in the institution's governance and representing the student body on various committees, they were positioned to address matters such as tuition increases or campus safety and thus did not see them as isolated issues. Per-

Table 6.2. Rankings of Most Important Student Government Services and Issues as Judged by Respondents in Government and Not in Government

Issue/Item	In Government	Not in Government
Rising tuition	8	1
Activities programming	3	2
Safety on campus	9	3
Race relations on campus	6[a]	4
Multicultural awareness and diversity	4	5[a]
Availability of classes	16	5[a]
Allocation of student activity fees	2	7
Allocation of university general funds	12	8
General student apathy	1	9
Sexual assualt and date rape	13	10
Participation in college or university governance	5	14
Representation on campuswide committees	6[a]	20[a]
Recycling and environmental issues	10	20[a]

[a] Item tied with another item.

haps the student government leaders were, by virtue of the range of issues with which they were involved, aware of a greater number of these issues than were the not-in-government students, who were most concerned with day-to-day matters such as tuition costs and safety. Thus, the student government respondents, as a group, may have been considering more choices as they indicated the most important items. However, it may also be the case that the student government leaders were, unfortunately, without knowledge of which matters were most important to their constituents.

These data also seem to indicate that the students outside the government believed that apathy was a concern, but not nearly to the same extent as their student government leaders, who ranked it as their most important matter. Apathy can be considered an important problem among government leaders for a number of reasons, including frustration over unsuccessful programs or activities. However, as discussed earlier in this chapter, the time and effort devoted to decrying apathy can be self-defeating for student government leaders. Not only do such efforts consume valuable time that might be used to address other matters, but to a constituency who perceives this issue as considerably less important, handwringing over apathy can make student government leaders appear ineffective in addressing other issues of greater concern to the general student body.

It is encouraging that in the present study there was relative agreement for three other items near the tops of both groups' lists. Activities programming was second among not-in-government students and third among in-government students, race relations on campus was fourth with the not-in-government students and tied for sixth on the in-government students' list, and multicultural awareness and diversity tied for fifth place among students not in government and was the fourth most frequent choice among student government members. Student government leaders not only should continue to keep these three issues as important agenda items but should also seek ways to integrate efforts that enhance race relations and diversity into the activities, programs, and events sponsored by student government.

The other response tied for fifth on the not-in-government list, availability of classes, was only the sixteenth most frequent answer given by student government members. And the issue of sexual assault and date rape, rounding out the top ten for the not-in-government students, was only thirteenth among their student government counterparts. Sexual assault and date rape, along with rising tuition and safety on campus, form a core of significant campus issues that the student government leaders in this study did not judge to be as important as did their constituents. One valuable lesson to be learned from these data may be that student government leaders ought to be certain that they are sufficiently attuned to student body opinions to know what those constituents deem important and to be willing to adapt their programs and resources to provide sufficient attention to those matters.

Three other issues that were among the top ten most frequently cited by student government members were ranked considerably lower by the not-in-government students. The fifth-ranked item among in-government students, participation in college or university governance, was only the fourteenth most frequent response among the not-in-government students. This difference is understandable since one of student government's raisons d'être is to represent the students in the institution's governance structure. Their constituents may assume that this representation is being attended to and do not consider it an important issue that requires their attention. So too with the issue of representation on campuswide committees, which tied for sixth among students in government but only tied for twentieth among not-in-government students. However, there is no obvious reason why the tenth most-frequent item on the list of student government members, recycling and environmental issues, was only tied for twentieth position among the students not in student government. Perhaps on some campuses recycling efforts have been successful enough to have met the needs of many of the student body members. Or maybe the students' reactions are similar to those of many members of society at large, who grudgingly admit that recycling is important but are not willing to invest the personal commitment required to make it work efficiently.

Conclusion

Throughout the history of higher education, student leaders have sought to provide services for their constituents. From the thirteenth-century student "nations," to the nineteenth-century literary societies, to the twentieth-century elected student governments, students have been providing that portion of the cocurriculum that the college or university administration has been unable, unwilling, or less efficiently inclined to produce.

From a sample of several hundred students, members and nonmembers of student government, a number of issues emerged as typical on a majority of campuses. For a number of these issues, however, there were concerns raised as to the effectiveness with which they were being addressed by student government. Among the issues yielding the most apparent disparities in perception were multicultural awareness and diversity and sexual assault and date rape. Diversity issues were being addressed on four out of five of the campuses represented in this study; but the percentage of students indicating that the issue was being met effectively was comparatively lower than that. The reverse was indicated for the issue of sexual assault; while one-third of the respondents in this study indicated that this issue was not being addressed at their campuses, three-fourths of those who did see some service being offered felt that it was effective.

The one issue with the greatest disparity between the perceptions of the two groups was general student apathy. Student government participants complain often about the general apathy of their constituents, a concern borne out by the in-government students' responses in this survey. Yet, those constituents are much less concerned with general apathy and, based on the not-in-government students' responses in this survey, seem primarily to want their student governments to address rising tuition and campus safety as well as to program cocurricular activities for them. Student government members seem to understand the need to program events and activities, but they do not appear to have heard the message about the other two most important issues. It appears that there is a breakdown in communication; whether the problem lies with the sender or the receiver, somehow the message is not getting through.

Another important finding of this study is that almost all of the items presented to the respondents were being addressed by some campuses. With the exception of only five issues, at least one-quarter of the respondents indicated that the other issues were being addressed on their campuses. Such matters as admissions standards, day care for students, graduation standards, and community homelessness were among the less "glamorous" issues receiving attention from some student governments. The data also demonstrate that some of the less popular issues can be addressed quite effectively by student government. Voter registration, legal aid services, office space for student organizations, and representation on administration search committees were several of the services not among the most prevalent on the list of issues, but they received relatively high ratings for effectiveness of delivery.

When the responses of students who were active in student government were compared to those of students not involved in student government, significant differences emerged, particularly in the perception of which services and issues were being addressed effectively and which were deemed most important to the campus community. Services as varied as registration of student organizations and membership on faculty search committees revealed statistically significant differences in the perceived effectiveness of their delivery by student government. Tuition increase, campus safety, and the availability of classes were several of the issues on which the two groups differed greatly in terms of how important they felt each of these matters was to the campus community. It is possible that not-in-government students lack the pertinent information to know truly the effectiveness or importance of these issues. Perchance, student government leaders tend toward self-service and assign importance to issues that are not that significant to the general student body whom these leaders are supposed to serve. Regardless of the reasons, the implications of such dissimilarities of perception can be quite important for student government leaders and their advisers.

The most important element in service delivery by student government is congruence between student leaders and their constituents as to the effectiveness of these services. Resources are too valuable to waste on ineffective work. Student government leaders also need to learn which issues the student body deems important to their lives. Effective communication among the student body is, perhaps, the student leaders' most precious resource.

Appendix: List of Issues on the Student Government Services Survey

1. Allocation of university general funds
2. Allocation of student activity fees
3. Rising tuition
4. Budget cuts
5. Enrollment ceilings
6. Textbook, computer, and instruction fees
7. Reduced availability of financial aid
8. Administrative and faculty salaries
9. Parking
10. Campus transit
11. Day care for students
12. Legal aid
13. Participation in on-campus housing services
14. Off-campus housing
15. Office space for student organizations
16. Safety on campus
17. AIDS and sexually transmitted diseases
18. Multicultural awareness and diversity
19. Admissions standards
20. Alcohol policy and alcohol abuse
21. Graduation standards
22. Availability of classes
23. Services for nontraditional and returning adult students
24. Organizing state or regional lobbies
25. Organizing national lobbies
26. Organizing local lobbies
27. Town-gown or community relations
28. Input on academic policy development
29. Participation in college or university governance
30. Representation on the college or university council or senate
31. Representation on campuswide committees
32. General student apathy
33. Input in faculty evaluation process
34. Faculty and staff collective bargaining
35. Representation on faculty search committees
36. Representation on administration search committees
37. Voter registration
38. Representation in community governance and special projects
39. Race relations on campus
40. Community homelessness
41. Rights of gays, lesbians, and bisexuals
42. Drug use and testing (including steroids)

43. Values and ethics
44. Sexual assault and date rape
45. Accessibility for the differently-abled
46. Recycling and environmental issues
47. Gender bias on campus
48. Recognition or registration of student organizations
49. Participation in judiciary (discipline)
50. Leading demonstrations and activism
51. Activities programming

References

Barr, M. J., Keating, L. A., and Associates. *Developing Effective Student Service Programs: Systematic Approaches for Practitioners.* San Francisco: Jossey-Bass, 1985.

Chiles, R., and Pruitt, D. "Student Associations: Viable Partners in Institutional Governance?" *Campus Activities Programming,* May 1985, pp. 21–24.

Cuyjet, M. "Student Government: The Nature of the Beast." *Campus Activities Programming,* May 1985, pp. 25–29.

Falvey, F. E. *Student Participation in College Administration.* New York: Teachers College Press, 1952.

Keppler, K., and Robinson, J. "Student Governments: What Are the Issues of the Day?" *Campus Activities Programming,* Apr. 1993, pp. 36–44.

Klopf, G. J. *College Student Government.* New York: HarperCollins, 1960.

Lunn, H. H. *The Student's Role in College Policy-Making.* Washington, D.C.: American Council on Education, 1957.

Saddlemire, G. L. "Student Activities." In A. L. Rentz and G. L. Saddlemire (eds.), *Student Affairs Functions in Higher Education.* Springfield, Ill.: Thomas, 1988.

MICHAEL J. CUYJET is associate professor in the Department of Educational and Counseling Psychology at the University of Louisville, Louisville, Kentucky. A former student affairs practitioner, he has served in campus activities and general student affairs capacities at several universities.

Development opportunities designed to clarify one's values and beliefs as part of an overall leadership training model will help meet one of society's most pressing needs: leadership rooted in the cultural value of improving the human condition for everyone.

Leadership Challenges, 2002

Dudley B. Woodard, Jr.

Imagine the demographic changes that will take place between now and the year 2002. The number of school children will climb to 53 million by the year 2002, surpassing the peak of 51.3 million in 1971. High school graduates will increase from 2.46 million to 2.88 million, and college graduates will be up from 14.1 million to 16 million by 2002. Minority enrollment is growing faster than white enrollment, and female enrollment at twice the rate of male enrollment (Evangelauf, 1992, p. A1).

Most likely, the trend of a low college enrollment rate for high school graduates from the lowest socioeconomic brackets will continue, and minority students will continue to drop out of college at higher rates than those of white students. And the participation rate of students in the age grouping of thirty-five and above will continue to increase (Andersen, 1990).

Four- and five-generation families living in single households will continue to increase as a percentage of the total population. The dependency rate of elderly (age sixty-five and older) to youth (infants to age seventeen) will almost be approximately the same by 2025 (Hodgkinson, 1989, p. 4). And the middle class will almost disappear as both the rich and the poor increase as percentages of total wealth distribution (Hodgkinson, 1989, p. 8).

These demographic and socioeconomic changes, coupled with technological changes, will dramatically alter our political systems, education constructs, cultures, and fundamental beliefs about quality of life. The issues and challenges for leaders of 2002 are today's seeds of racism, violence, substance abuse, neglect of youth, and underprepared students. The question becomes whether or not today's youth are being readied to meet these leadership challenges and their consequences. This chapter addresses these issues in detail, including the leadership development requisite to meet the challenges, and offers suggestions to prepare today's leaders for tomorrow's challenges.

The Leadership Challenge

In Alice Walker's novel *The Temple of My Familiar,* Fanny's mother Olivia declares, "To me all daily stories are in fact ancient, and ancient ones current. I've grown to know that there is nothing new under the sun and that nothing in the past is more mysterious than the behavior of the present." John McGuire, president of the Claremont Graduate School, has used Olivia's observation to make the point that "the more things change the more they stay the same . . . however different and novel our times and their challenges *seem* to be, they're not that different from the issues and conundrums our forebears had to wrestle" (McGuire, 1989, p. 2).

Leadership has been a source of fascination and misunderstanding for millennia and remains an enigma that no single theory can fully explain. There are varying views on what constitutes a good leader, but agreement exists that there is a leadership crisis in our country. Many leaders are perceived as driven by self-interest and profit rather than by the common good. The visionary power of the voices of Martin Luther King, Jr., Golda Meir, and John F. Kennedy is gone, replaced by those whom Bennis (1989, p. 36) described as "McHeroes," such as Ivan Boesky, Oliver North, and Pete Rose.

The data collected on entering freshmen each year under the Cooperative Institutional Research Program clearly show fundamental shifts over the past several years in attitudes and beliefs among today's college-age students. Some of the findings are that (1) test scores have dropped but high school grades are higher; (2) the fields of engineering, business, and computer science have increased in popularity while the appeal of traditional liberal arts has decreased significantly; and (3) today's student is interested in "being very well-off financially" and less interested in "developing a meaningful philosophy of life" (Astin, 1985, p. 216). As Astin (1985, p. 217) observed, "Most of the values given higher priority in recent years are concerned with money, power, and status; being very well off financially, being an authority, having administrative responsibility for others, and winning recognition. . . . These value changes are highly consistent with the changes in student majors and career plans. Increased student interest in business, engineering, and computer science has been accompanied by a strengthening of materialistic and power values, whereas decreased student interest in education, social science, the arts, the humanities, nursing, social work, allied health, and the clergy has been accompanied by a decline in altruism and social concern."

A look toward the immediate future may well reveal a world much like the one presented in Richard Linklater's movie *Slacker*—a generation of disinterested youth who believe that they have been abandoned by the system and by the preceding generations, leaving them with little opportunity and hope. These youth, together with a rapidly aging majority population, produce a bleak picture. Have the dreams been lost? Are the dreamers gone? Are today's emerging voices of leadership (the baby boomers) crying "Me" rather than "Us"? Is this X generation a bunch of whiners rather than doers?

Our nation is facing great challenges in areas such as racism, neglect of youth, violence, health care, underpreparation of students, environmental concerns, competition in a global economy, and the need for enlightened, altruistic leadership. Where will we find these leaders?

Shifting Leadership Paradigm

The research on student leadership has focused mainly on leadership development and skill development programs instead of the task of designing opportunities for leadership, anchored in leadership and organizational theories. Birnbaum (1989, p. 126) noted that "with few exceptions . . . studies of leadership in higher education have been theoretical and, for the most part, not explicitly grounded in the organizational leadership literature." A content review of student leadership development programs (Harshbarger, 1988; McIntire, 1989; Ritter and Brown, 1986; Roberts and Ullom, 1989; Striffolino and Saunders, 1989) reveals an emphasis on the development of skills such as assertiveness, problem solving, conflict management, organization, and decision making, with an increasing emphasis on "the development of values and ethics regarding their use" (Harshbarger, 1988, p. 108). Leaders have been seen more in terms of dichotomous variables: "authoritarian or participative, bureaucratic or collegial, transformational or transactional, task or people oriented" (Bensimon, Neumann, and Birnbaum, 1989, p. 70).

Critics state that these approaches to student leadership development are not actually leadership development but instead leadership credentialing. Irving J. Spitzburg, of the Association of American Colleges, believes that "true leadership programs involve considerations of the nature of government and society. By discussing the type of leaders we want and the nature of the leadership, we are in fact discussing what sort of society we want to live in. Lacking these elements, leadership has a propensity to become a Yuppie development program" (Hirschhorn, 1988, p. A41).

Because organizations have become so complex and because societal issues such as poverty, substance abuse, and violence are overwhelming the systems designed to combat these problems, an increasing number of scholars and leaders are calling for different approaches to student leadership development. Bensimon, Neumann, and Birnbaum (1989) presented an integrated perspective of leadership. They concluded that there is no single leadership theory or organizational theory that is right or complete; rather, leadership must be viewed from multiple leadership and organizational theories. The effective leader understands these approaches and uses them in ways that depend on the characteristics of the people, needs, setting, and organizational structure.

As Birnbaum (1989, p. 134) stated, "It may be a mistake to believe that all leadership must come from 'leaders.' In many institutions, much of the required guidance and support may be provided by the participants, the nature of the task, or the characteristics of the organizations itself." Future leaders will have to abandon past stereotypes about effective leadership and unlearn past behavior and beliefs in order to be effective in an increasingly complex and pluralistic society.

Most of today's leadership theories (for example, transactional, transformational, situational, and symbolic leadership) and styles emerged after World War II, fueled by the public's belief that there has been a failure of leadership in government, education, and business. According to Bensimon, Neumann, and Birnbaum (1989), there are six major categories of theories: (1) Trait theories describe individual characteristics believed to be associated with successful leadership. Power and influence perspectives examine the source and use of power by leaders. Behavioral theories study leaders' patterns of activities and roles under different conditions. Contingency theories emphasize the importance of the environment—the contextual setting or situational factors. Cultural and symbolic theories represent the "influence of leaders in maintaining or reinterpreting the system of shared beliefs and values that give meaning to organizational life" (Bensimon, Neumann, and Birnbaum, 1989, p. 7). Cognitive theories suggest that leadership is a "social attribution that permits people to make sense of an equivocal, fluid, and complex world" (Bensimon, Neumann, and Birnbaum, 1989, p. 7). (2) There are also several organizational models, such as the classic bureaucratic or rational models. Bolman and Deal's model (1991) has attracted great interest because it allows individuals to look through different lenses as a way of interpreting events and behavior and organizing activities (see Bolman and Deal, 1984). (3) The structural frame "emphasizes the importance of formal roles and relationships" (Bolman and Deal, 1991, p. 15). "Leaders hold the foremost role in decision making, analyzing problems, determining alternate solutions, choosing the best one and executing it" (Bensimon, Neumann, and Birnbaum, 1989, p. 33). (4) The human relations frame views organizations "as collectives with organizational members as their primary resource. The emphasis is on human needs and how organizations can be tailored to meet them" (Bensimon, Neumann, and Birnbaum, 1989, p. 33). (5) The political frame sees organizations as "formal and informal groups vying for power to control institutional processes and outcomes. Decisions arise from bargaining, influencing, and coalition building" (Bensimon, Neumann, and Birnbaum, 1989, p. 33). And (6) the symbolic frame views organizations as "loosely coupled and as having ambiguous goals" (Bensimon, Neumann, and Birnbaum, 1989, p. 33). Organizational structures and processes are invented depending on the context and culture (Bensimon, Neumann, and Birnbaum, 1989, p. 33; Bolman and Deal, 1991, p. 15).

Need for New and Multiple Leadership Approaches

The current trend for institutions to develop leadership programs reflects a national yearning for more effective government. Leadership development is what is needed to stem the ongoing ethical, political, and economic decline in the United States (Hirschhorn, 1988). As a nation, we seem to be experiencing a fundamental shift in values and beliefs. American youth are moving away from values centered around helping others to values of personal acquisition and pleasure. Unfortunately, this change does not seem to be cyclical but rather represents a fundamental societal shift (Astin, 1985). It is this change in the values of the youth that must be addressed as part of an overall approach to preparing young people for leadership positions both in this country and in the international arena.

Harshbarger (1988, p. 108) reflected this belief in stating that "to learn behavioral skills applicable to leadership without initiating the development of values and ethics regarding their use, is at best fruitless and at worst, dangerous." Leaders lead from their values and beliefs. Development opportunities designed to clarify one's values and beliefs as part of an overall leadership training model will help meet one of society's most pressing needs: leadership rooted in the cultural value of improving the human condition for everyone. This is accomplished by examining today's cultural assumptions and tomorrow's needs, and determining what changes must be made in order to be in a position to meet those ends. To meet the needs of tomorrow, institutions must challenge students to examine their values so that they understand what will be required of them in order to mobilize society and tackle these needs. Some of these future issues are as follows.

Neglect of Youth. Approximately one-fourth of our children live in poverty. That figure approaches nearly one-half for African American and Hispanic children (Atwell, 1991, pp. 2–3). A poor child is more likely than a non-poor child to go without food, shelter, and health care; to die in infancy; to drop out of school; to get pregnant too soon; and to be unemployed (Basha, 1991).

Racism Tearing at Society's Quilt. Racism is tearing our cities apart and has reared its ugly head on many campuses. The evidence of disintegration is well documented by the stark differences in graduation rates and incomes between whites and Hispanics, African Americans, and Native Americans (Atwell, 1991).

A Political System in Crisis. Greed and self-interest have replaced altruism and duty to care in business and government. The excessive dependence of our political leaders on major donors and political action committees has blinded them to the ideal of public service and placed them on a path of betrayal of the public trust. The lack of ethics, disregard for others as individuals, and blatant misuse of power have caused a collapse of confidence in America's leaders.

Environment. The environment continues to decay as measured by air quality in our cities, overreliance on fossil fuels, and the destruction of our forests and wetlands (Atwell, 1991).

Educational Anomie. The public has lost confidence in our schools. Our system has declined to such a degree that our children have fallen behind students in other nations with which we compete economically. The term *educational leadership* is seen as an oxymoron (Atwell, 1991).

Economic Stratification. The middle class is shrinking rapidly. In the decades from 1940 to 1990, the middle class comprised approximately 80 percent of the U.S. population. Currently, there is a "squeezing" trend. The middle class is now only 60 percent of the population, with the slack taken up by the upper and lower classes (Hodgkinson, 1989).

Substance Abuse. Treatment programs, interventions, and attempts at reducing supplies have not had much effect in deterring substance abuse. Alcohol and drugs are clearly linked to the increasing violence in our cities, and this increase in abuse and violence shows no signs of abatement.

These represent some of the challenges facing our future leaders. The leaders of tomorrow must be educated about these issues, grounded in humanistic values, and trained in the skills that will help them tackle these problems.

Leadership 2002 Model

What is leadership? Is it hierarchical or heterarchical? Is it directing and controlling or collaborative and empowering? In order to understand the concept of leadership, what it really is, we must first understand what leadership is not. It is not management, but the ability to manage is part of leadership. It is not the unbridled use of power, but power is an element of leadership. It is not manipulation, but leadership involves the influencing of behavior. It is not self-serving, but leadership serves the interests of the group.

According to Maccoby (1979, p. 20), leadership is serving and empowering people, building trust, facilitating cooperation, and explaining the "significance of the individual's role in the common purpose." If we are to bring out our full potential, we must focus on the positive aspects of human character and work toward establishing a moral code that meets the common need and appeals to the common good (Maccoby, 1979). We can no longer afford to follow false prophets who lure us away from building our community and steer us toward self-serving goals.

The next generation of leaders in the United States must move forward, embracing change but balancing it with concern for humanistic values. They may not be heroes in the popular definition, but they will be mindful of and proficient in relationship building. They will be able to assess and adapt to situations, utilizing a variety of techniques to help others understand and transmit their vision. They will be decisive, competent, flexible, and comfortable with risk taking. They will understand that leadership is not static; it is meant to be shared, so they will pass on their knowledge and skills to the next generation. They will remember that to be a leader means, especially, having the opportunity to make a meaningful difference in the lives of those who permit leaders to lead (DePree, 1981).

To achieve these goals, faculty and student affairs practitioners need to work collaboratively to define and create opportunities for students to learn more about leadership and participate in activities that enhance leadership development. Leadership development should not be primarily focused on visible campus student leaders or centered in student government activities; rather, it should be seen as an opportunity to involve many students in activities both on and off campus.

The following guidelines, based on the work of Roberts and Ullom (1989), are recommended in the planning of leadership development opportunities:

Theory. Students should be exposed to different leadership and organizational theories. The purpose is to help students understand the interactive nature of setting leadership tasks and that examining the task and setting through multiple lenses deepens understanding, leading to differentiated responses depending on the characteristics of a given situation. Students can be exposed to organizational and leadership theory in a variety of ways: formal classes, leadership programs sponsored by student affairs, seminars and speaker series, and ongoing orientation programs. This step is the requisite building block for an effective leadership development program.

Values Clarification. As stated earlier, current trends in values run counter to the values that will be needed to provide enlightened and effective leadership for 2002. As educators, we sometimes assume that students will be exposed to and adopt the values we believe are central to sustaining our vision of society. Unfortunately, the evidence is quite clear—today's students are more materialistic oriented rather than committed to a way of life which will help tackle the problems besetting society. College or university faculty, administrators, and student personnel practitioners must create opportunities for values clarification and development as a way of developing an understanding of the values necessary to help solve societal problems.

Skills Development. Students need to be given opportunities to develop skills in areas such as social activism, conflict resolution, collaborative learning, and constituency building, along with the more traditional skills of decision making, judgment, and communication.

Societal Issues. Students must be exposed to the major societal challenges and the types of leadership needed to address these issues. Information sessions, debates, and speakers are some ways to inform students and inspire them to think creatively about how these issues can be tackled by their generation.

Experience. In order for students to gain confidence and reflect on their experiences, leadership opportunities need to be created that will allow students to test their notions of leadership and gain valuable feedback. Faculty and student affairs practitioners should work together to create leadership opportunities on and off campus. In designing these opportunities, it is important to provide students with mentors. If we are serious about changing the direction of leadership and society, then we need to invest the human resources necessary and be proactive in planning and coordinating these activities.

"'I know,' said Winter, 'but they don't know.' And he went on with a thought he had been having. 'A time-minded people,' he said, 'and the time is nearly up. They think that just because they have only one leader and one head, we are all like that. They know that ten heads lopped off will destroy them, but we are a free people; we have as many heads as we have people, and in a time of need leaders pop up among us like mushrooms'" (Steinbeck, 1942, p. 175).

References

Andersen, C. J. *Enrollment by Age: Distinguishing the Numbers from the Rates.* Research Brief No. 7. Washington, D.C.: Division of Policy Analysis and Research, American Council on Education, 1990.

Astin, A. W. *Achieving Educational Excellence: A Critical Assessment of Priorities and Practices in Higher Education.* San Francisco: Jossey-Bass, 1985.

Atwell, R. H. "Opening the American Mind: Fairness, Consensus, and the Role of the Academy." Paper presented at the annual meeting of the American Council on Education, San Francisco, Jan. 1991.

Basha, E. "The Unfinished Agenda: Arizona Children in Need." Paper presented at the Children's Action Alliance, Tucson, Arizona, Oct. 1991.

Bennis, W. *Why Leaders Can't Lead: The Unconscious Conspiracy Continues.* San Francisco: Jossey-Bass, 1989.

Bensimon, E. M., Neumann, A., and Birnbaum, R. *Making Sense of Administrative Leadership: The "L" Word in Higher Education.* ASHE-ERIC Higher Education Reports, no. 1. Washington, D.C.: Association for the Study of Higher Education, 1989.

Birnbaum, R. "The Implicit Leadership Theories of College and University Presidents." *Review of Higher Education,* 1989, *12* (2), 125–136.

Bolman, L. G., and Deal, T. E. *Modern Approaches to Understanding and Managing Organizations.* San Francisco: Jossey-Bass, 1984.

Bolman, L. G., and Deal, T. E. *Reframing Organizations: Artistry, Choice, and Leadership.* San Francisco: Jossey-Bass, 1991.

DePree, M. *Leadership Is an Art.* New York: Dell, 1989.

Evangelauf, J. "Enrollment Projections Revised Upward in New Government Analysis." *Chronicle of Higher Education,* Jan. 22, 1992, pp. A1, A36.

Harshbarger, B. "A Framework for Student Leadership Development Programs." In *Student Services, Responding to Issues and Challenges: The Fifth Compendium of Papers by Student Services Officers of the University of North Carolina.* Chapel Hill: University of North Carolina, 1988. (ED 299 896)

Hirschhorn, M. W. " 'Leadership' Programs, with Doses of Self-Absorption and Idealism, Strike Responsive Chord in Students." *Chronicle of Higher Education,* Apr. 13, 1988, pp. A39–A41.

Hodgkinson, H. L. *The Same Client: The Demographics of Education and Service Delivery Systems.* Washington, D.C.: Center for Demographic Policy, Institute for Educational Leadership, 1989.

Maccoby, M. "Leadership Needs of the 1980s." *Current Issues in Higher Education,* 1979, *1,* 17–23. (ED 193 997)

McGuire, J. "Vision, Values, and Voices: Creating Our World Anew." Keynote address presented at the annual meeting of the National Association of Student Personnel Administrators, Richard F. Stevens Institute, Oakland, California, July 1989.

McIntire, D. D. "Student Leadership Development: A Student Affairs Mandate." *NASPA Journal,* 1989, *27* (1), 75–79.

Ritter, D. A., and Brown, M. L. *Considerations for the Development of Leadership Programs in Higher Education.* Columbia: University of South Carolina/Omaha, Nebr.: Creighton University, 1986. (ED 278 289)

Roberts, D., and Ullom, C. "Student Leadership Program Model." *NASPA Journal,* 1989, *27* (1), 67–74.

Steinbeck, J. *The Moon Is Down.* New York: Viking, 1942.

Striffolino, P., and Saunders, S. A. "Emerging Leaders: Students in Need of Development." *NASPA Journal,* 1989, *27* (1), 51–58.

DUDLEY B. WOODARD, JR., is a professor at the Center for the Study of Higher Education, University of Arizona, Tucson. He is former vice president of student affairs at the University of Arizona and a past president of NASPA.

This chapter presents a synopsis of the major ideas and conclusions of this volume and a short annotated bibliography of several important sources used by the authors.

Conclusions and Annotated Bibliography

Michael J. Cuyjet, Melvin C. Terrell

Effective college or university governance requires the cooperative, collaborative effort of administrators, faculty, and students, each representing a different perspective in the campus milieu. Effective participation by students in this governance process generally requires an accepted structure and systematic procedure for their contributions; the need for a structure is fulfilled by student government. Effective student government on the campus requires not just a body of willing, responsible students but the dedication and commitment of student affairs staff to support, guide, and motivate those students who participate in the process of campus governance.

In order to maximize the effects of the relationship between student affairs staff and the student leaders with whom they work, advisers must help students transcend the common transactional traits of management by control, domination, and manipulation of rewards so as to lead with charisma, inspirational motivation, intellectual stimulation, and individualized consideration. Student affairs staff need to understand students' motives, their agendas, their foci, and the stress they encounter. Staff must work with student leaders to help them achieve their goals and realize personal growth in the process. Above all, this relationship must be ethical, both in the work that they do together and as a teaching medium for training students to behave ethically in all of their actions. Integrity, honesty, commitment, and an ethic of care are all essential components of a model code of ethics.

Participation in student government is more than just a cocurricular activity; it is the fulfillment of expectations of good citizenship. Student government can also provide exposure to the views and ideas of others who are different from oneself. Student government affords a chance to practice skills such as organizing, planning, managing, and decision making and opportunities to synthesize and integrate material from classes, laboratories, and studios.

As participants in an institution's governance, student government leaders provide constituents with services and support. On a majority of campuses, the prevalent student government roles include service as official representative to the institution's collective governance body and on campuswide committees, activities programming, allocation of student fees, and recognition or registration of student organizations, although the variety of services is as broad as the number of schools offering them. It is important to note also that students who are active in government and those who are not active differ in their perceptions of the importance of some issues and services.

Student affairs staff are challenged to accomplish the dual tasks of helping ethnically diverse students achieve parity in their leadership roles and teaching all student leaders to be sensitive to the factors that can diminish multicultural participation in student government and to work to eliminate them. To accomplish these tasks, student affairs personnel who work with student government leaders must model an empathetic understanding of the needs of ethnically diverse student leaders and provide support to students who indicate that they have not had the same mainstream leadership opportunities as members of the predominant culture. If a leader is someone who motivates others to effect change, student activism is a legitimate form of student leadership, either within student government or through other organizations. Activism is also an important part of students' learning experiences, as they choose to act on their social and political commitments and to exert influence in the institutional milieu.

In order to be effective leaders for the future, students need an understanding of different leadership and organizational theories. They must develop skills in values clarification, collaborative learning, and constituency building, as well as traditional organizational skills of communication, decision making, and conflict resolution. Students must also be helped to confront constructively the societal challenges they will face and provided with the freedom and encouragement needed to be creative in deriving solutions to these problems. These are among the challenges facing student affairs personnel who have the responsibility of shaping the behaviors of the student government leaders of today and tomorrow.

This volume is not intended to be a scholarly approach to the matters facing student government leaders. Rather, it is an outline of some of the major issues related to this population and a guide for those involved in such matters on our campuses to understand the dynamics of student government leadership. In several areas, including personal gains achieved, services provided, and participation by ethnically diverse students, students' perceptions are incorporated into the presentations here. It is the authors' intentions to stimulate thinking, to provide helpful ideas and concepts, and to motivate both staff and students to greater productivity through enhanced relationships.

The following sources were particularly useful to the authors in the formulation of their ideas:

Barr, M. J., and Associates. *The Handbook of Student Affairs Administration.* San Francisco: Jossey-Bass, 1993.

This book contains, in one volume, practically everything student affairs administrators need to know about the profession. In thirty-six chapters, leading student affairs experts present important information regarding the philosophy, policies, practices, procedures, and principles that are vital to the understanding and implementation of student affairs work in the current era and for the new millennium. This book unifies and systematizes every important aspect of professional practice.

Barr, M. J., Keating, L. A., and Associates. *Developing Effective Student Services Programs: Systematic Approaches for Practitioners.* San Francisco: Jossey-Bass, 1985.

This book takes a comprehensive look at program planning, development, and implementation. Beginning with the preplanning aspects of determining how programs fit into the institutional context and the process of goal setting, the book proceeds to outline the important steps for implementing quality programs: systematic planning, developing competent staff, establishing quality, and maintaining utility over time. The volume also describes common pitfalls and ways to avoid or correct them.

Kuh, G. D., Schuh, J. H., Whitt, E. J., and Associates. *Involving Colleges: Successful Approaches to Fostering Student Learning and Development Outside the Classroom.* San Francisco: Jossey-Bass, 1991.

Utilizing qualitative research methods, this book examines the out-of-class environments of fourteen colleges and universities that provide unusually rich learning experiences for students. The book concludes with recommendations for student affairs professionals and faculty members interested in enhancing the out-of-class learning environments on their campuses.

Pascarella, E. T., and Terenzini, P. T. *How College Affects Students: Findings and Insights from Twenty Years of Research.* San Francisco: Jossey-Bass, 1991.

This comprehensive volume reviews twenty-six hundred research studies on the effects of college on students. The contributions of out-of-class experiences to student learning and personal development are considered in areas such as verbal, quantitative, and subject matter competence; cognitive skills and intellectual growth; identity, self concept, and self-esteem; relating to others; attitudes and values; moral development; educational attainment; and career choice and development.

Terrell, M. C. (ed.). *Diversity, Disunity, and Campus Community*. Washington, D.C.: National Association of Student Personnel Administrators, 1992.

This book helps university leaders address student diversity "by acquiring the necessary skills and vision to create and nurture a campus climate conducive to living and learning for the new student population" (p. xii). The monograph provides information on current trends and pressures facing our institutions with respect to diversity and offers pragmatic advice on these cutting-edge issues.

Vellela, T. *New Voices: Student Activism in the Eighties and Nineties*. Boston: South End Press, 1988.

The book describes today's student activists as people ready to challenge the current systems and to move beyond the institutionalized roadblocks to significant change. Graduate and undergraduate students at twenty-three institutions were interviewed and activist students at more than one hundred other campuses were surveyed to measure the impact of campus political activism. The book opens with a chapter presenting a global perspective on worldwide activism and includes chapters on divestment, Central America, the Central Intelligence Agency, racism, women's issues, gay, lesbian, and bisexual rights, and the role of the media.

MICHAEL J. CUYJET *is associate professor in the Department of Educational and Counseling Psychology at the University of Louisville, Louisville, Kentucky. A former student affairs practitioner, he has served in campus activities and general student affairs capacities at several universities.*

MELVIN C. TERRELL *is vice president for student affairs and professor of counselor education at Northeastern Illinois University, Chicago. He was a 1993–1994 American Council on Education Fellow at Florida State University.*

INDEX

Ordering Information

New Directions for Student Services is a series of paperback books that offers guidelines and programs for aiding students in their total development—emotional, social, and physical, as well as intellectual. Books in the series are published quarterly in spring, summer, fall, and winter and are available for purchase by subscription as well as by single copy.

Subscriptions for 1994 cost $47.00 for individuals (a savings of 25 percent over single-copy prices) and $62.00 for institutions, agencies, and libraries. Please do not send institutional checks for personal subscriptions. Standing orders are accepted.

Single copies cost $15.95 when payment accompanies order. (California, New Jersey, New York, and Washington, D.C., residents please include appropriate sales tax.) Billed orders will be charged postage and handling.

Discounts for quantity orders are available. Please write to the address below for information.

All orders must include either the name of an individual or an official purchase order number. Please submit your order as follows:
  Subscriptions: specify series and year subscription is to begin
  Single copies: include individual title code (such as SS55)

Mail all orders to:
  Jossey-Bass Publishers
  350 Sansome Street
  San Francisco, California 94104-1342

OTHER TITLES AVAILABLE IN THE
NEW DIRECTIONS FOR STUDENT SERVICES SERIES
Margaret J. Barr, Editor-in-Chief
M. Lee Upcraft, Associate Editor